# Deliver Your Message:

## Enhancing Presentation Skills with Videographics

Makoto Shishido

Mariko Takahashi

Kevin Murphy

JN215226

**SEIBIDO**

## StreamLine

### Web 動画・音声ファイルのストリーミング再生について

CD マーク及び Web 動画マークがある箇所は、PC、スマートフォン、タブレット端末において、無料でストリーミング再生することができます。下記 URL よりご利用ください。再生手順や動作環境などは本書巻末の「Web 動画のご案内」をご覧ください。

**https://st.seibido.co.jp**

### 音声ファイルのダウンロードについて

CD マークがある箇所は、ダウンロードすることも可能です。下記 URL の書籍詳細ページにあるダウンロードアイコンをクリックしてください。

**https://seibido.co.jp/ad715**

## Deliver Your Message:
### Enhancing Presentation Skills with Videographics

# はじめに

　本書は、プレゼンテーションスキルを向上させたい学生のために作成された教科書です。プレゼンテーションに初めて取り組む学生にも、スキルを強化したい学生にも、この教科書は包括的なガイダンスと実践的な練習を提供しています。今日の世界では、強力なプレゼンテーションスキルが不可欠です。これらのスキルは、学業、キャリア、日常のコミュニケーションで成功するのに役立ちます。本書は、アイディアの計画と構築から、パワーポイントなどの視覚提示を利用して聴衆を引き込む方法、自信を持って話す方法まで、プレゼンテーションのすべての側面をカバーしています。

　学生が興味を引くような、身近な社会の話題について、ビデオグラフィックスの映像を通じたリスニングやスピーキングの演習を利用し、基礎的な英語能力の向上をめざします。さらには、英語での発想力や基本的なプレゼンテーション構成能力を高め、発表するための英語表現力を養成することを主眼とした、中級者向けの教材です。

　本書では、効果的なプレゼンテーションを行うための基礎を学ぶために、Pre-Unit を設けています。この Pre-Unit では、プレゼンテーションの目的設定、聴衆の理解、構成の作成、内容の整理、スライドデザイン、スピーチの準備、身振りや表情の活用、質疑応答の準備、リハーサルの重要性など、プレゼンテーションの成功に不可欠な要素について段階的に説明しています。これにより、学生はプレゼンテーションのスキルを体系的に習得し、実践に役立てることができます。

　本書の構成は下記のような特徴を持っています。

I. **Warm-up**：ビデオグラフィックスの映像を視聴する前に、基礎的な知識や語彙力を確認する演習を行います。

  1. **Opening Questions**：各課の話題について学生の知識や興味を問うトップダウン形式の質問です。

  2. **Vocabulary Study**：ビデオグラフィックスで利用されている単語について、英語と日本語の意味を一致させる形式の練習問題です。

  3. **Vocabulary Practice**：ビデオグラフィックスで利用されている単語について、選択肢から適切な単語を選ぶ、空所補充形式の練習問題です。

II. **Listening**：本書の中心となる各課の話題を紹介するビデオグラフィックスの映像を視聴し、リスニング能力を向上させるためのさまざまな演習に取り組みます。

  1. **Note Taking**：ビデオグラフィックスの映像を見て、要旨を簡潔にまとめる演習です。効果的なプレゼンテーションを行うためには話すことだけでなく、積極的に聞くことも重要です。本書には、他の人のプレゼンテーションの重要なポイントを理解し、記憶するために効率的にノートを取る方法も含まれています。

  2. **Comprehension Questions**：映像で紹介されている内容についての理解を確認する、T/F 形式の問題です。

**III. Speaking**：プレゼンテーションを行う前段階の発話能力の向上を目指した演習です。

1. **Speaking Practice**：各課の話題についての賛成や反対の意見を述べる、会話形式のスピーキング演習です。
2. **Create a Dialog**：ペアワークで会話を考え、発話練習を行います。プレゼンテーションにはしばしば、質疑応答やディスカッションが含まれます。これらのやり取りに関して、自信を持ち、質問やコメントに効果的に対応できるように練習します。

**IV. Presentation**：プレゼンテーションを作成し、実践的な発表ができるように演習を行います。

1. **Research**：プレゼンテーションの話題について調べ、必要な情報、知識を獲得します。
2. **Brainstorming**：プレゼンテーションを作成する上で元となるアイディアを整理するためには、ブレインストーミングでさまざまな考えを書き出すことが重要です。
3. **Organizing**：書き出したアイディアを整理し、論理的な構成に組み立てます。成功するプレゼンテーションには計画が重要です。また、これらのステップに従うことで、プレゼンテーションの内容を明確で論理的な流れにまとめることができます。
4. **Presenting**：実際にプレゼンテーションを行います。

**コラム (Presentationのヒント)**：プレゼンテーション能力を向上させるためのコツや注意点などをわかりやすくまとめています。

巻末付録
1. プレゼンテーションの評価シート (Presentation Evaluation Rubric/Sheets)
2. 論理展開例・表現例
   2-1 **プレゼンテーションの論理展開例**：プレゼンテーションの本論を構成するためのいくつかの論理的な展開例を提供しています。年代順、問題解決、原因と結果など、さまざまなアプローチを取ることができる例やテンプレートを見ることができます。これらのパターンにより、プレゼンテーションが一貫して説得力のあるものになります。
   2-2 **論理展開別有用表現**：オープニングとクロージング：聴衆に対して最初の印象と継続的な影響を与えるには、オープニングとクロージングの発言で決まります。聴衆の注意を引くためのさまざまなテクニックと、強力で記憶に残る結論を残すための方法を提案しています。

　この教科書がプレゼンテーションスキルを向上させるための貴重なリソースとなることを願っています。提供された技術や戦略を実践し、応用することで、より自信を持ち、効果的なプレゼンターになることができるようになります。本書を利用して、プレゼンテーションを楽しんでください。

著者一同

# EnglishCentralのご案内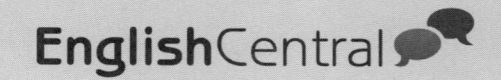

　本テキスト各ユニットの「II LISTENING」と「III SPEAKING」の「1 SPEAKING PRACTICE」で学習する動画と音声は、オンライン学習システム「EnglishCentral」で学習することができます。

　EnglishCentralでは動画の視聴や単語のディクテーションのほか、動画のセリフを音読し録音すると、コンピュータが発音を判定します。PCのwebだけでなく、スマートフォン、タブレットではアプリでも学習できます。リスニング、スピーキング、語彙力向上のため、ぜひ活用してください。

　EnglishCentralの利用にはアカウントとアクセスコードの登録が必要です。登録方法については下記ページにアクセスしてください。

（画像はすべてサンプルで、実際の教材とは異なります）

**https://www.seibido.co.jp/englishcentral/pdf/ectextregister.pdf**

**見る**

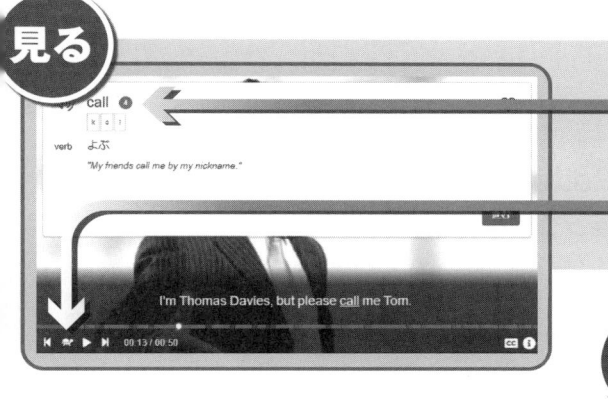

**本文内でわからなかった単語は1クリックでその場で意味を確認**

**スロー再生**

**学ぶ**

**音声を聴いて空欄の単語をタイピング。ゲーム感覚で楽しく単語を覚える**

**話す**

**動画のセリフを音読し録音、コンピュータが発音を判定。**

**日本人向けに専門開発された音声認識によってスピーキング力を%で判定**

**ネイティブと自分が録音した発音を聞き比べ練習に生かすことができます**

**苦手な発音記号を的確に判断し、単語を緑、黄、赤の3色で表示**

# CONTENTS

**Unit 1**

## Facial Recognition: What's in a Face?

顔認証技術の利便性と危険性

**Unit 2**

## Daylight Saving Time

サマータイムは省エネにつながる

**Unit 3**

## How Fashion Pollutes

おしゃれはファッション公害を引き起こす

**Unit 4**

## Interest Rates

経済を活性化するために有効な金利政策とは？

**Unit 5**

## Artificial Intelligence

人工知能を有効に活用するために

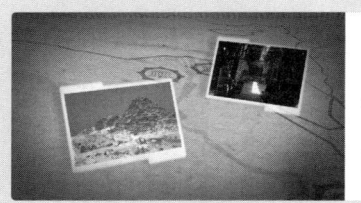

**Unit 6**

## World Heritage Sites

文化の多様性を保護する世界遺産

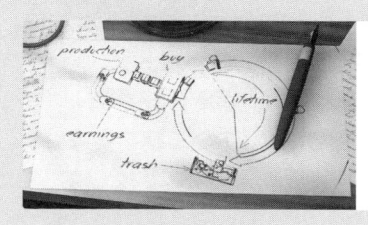

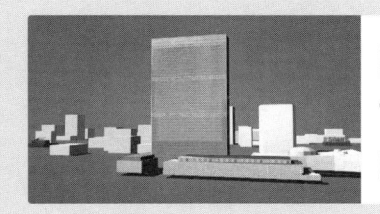

# Pre-Unit ▶ プレゼンテーションの概要と準備

## Ⅰ プレゼンテーションとは

プレゼンテーションとは、あるテーマに関して、聴衆に対して情報やアイディアを伝えるために口頭発表を行うことです。主にビジネス、学術、教育、広報などさまざまな分野で行われます。プレゼンテーションは、コミュニケーションスキルの重要な側面であり、ビジネスや学術分野で成功するために必要なスキルの一つです。プレゼンテーションを成功させるために、以下の事柄を参考にしましょう。

**Point 1** **目的を明確にする**

プレゼンテーションの目的をはっきりさせることが重要です。何を伝えたいのか、聴衆にどんなアクションを促したいのかを明確にし、準備を進めましょう。

**Point 2** **聴衆を理解する**

聴衆のニーズや興味を理解することが成功の鍵です。誰が聴衆なのか、どのような背景を持っているのかを考慮して内容を選択します。

**Point 3** **プレゼンテーションの構成を決める**

プレゼンテーションの骨子となる構成を考えます。典型的な構成は以下の通りです。

1. Introduction（プレゼンの目的や自己紹介）
   ↓
2. Body（重要なポイントやデータの提示）
   ↓
3. Conclusion（まとめや結論）
   ↓
4. Q&A（質疑応答：聴衆からの質問に対する対応）

**Point 4** **内容を整理する**

主となる内容を適切な順序で整理します。論理的な流れを持たせることで、聴衆は理解しやすくなります。

**Point 5** **簡潔さ・明確さを重視する**

スライドやスピーチの内容は簡潔で明確に表現します。長文は避け、キーポイントを強調しましょう。また、専門用語を避け、わかりやすい言葉で説明することも大切です。

### Point 6 　資料のデザインを考える

視覚的な要素も重要です。シンプルで分かりやすいスライドデザイン、適切なフォントや色の選択、画像やグラフの挿入などを検討します。

### Point 7 　スピーチの準備をする

スライドだけでなく、スピーチの内容やトーンも重要です。練習を重ねて、自信を持ってプレゼンテーションを行えるようにします。

### Point 8 　身振りや表情を活用する

言葉だけでなく、身振り、手振り（ジェスチャー）や表情を使って、説明を補完しましょう。

### Point 9 　質疑応答の準備

質疑応答に備えて、予想される質問や不確かな点についての答えを準備しておきます。

### Point 10 　リハーサルを行う

完成したプレゼンテーションを何度かリハーサルしましょう。時間配分、タイミング、表現を確認し、改善の余地があるかを見つけます。

### Point 11 　フィードバックを受ける

他の人にプレゼンテーションを見てもらい、フィードバックを受けることで、さらなる改善点を見つけることができます。

これらの方法を活用して、プレゼンテーションをより効果的で魅力的なものにすることができます。継続的な改善と練習を通じて、プレゼンテーションのスキルを向上させましょう。

## II プレゼンテーションの準備

## 1 Brainstorming（ブレインストーミング）

ブレインストーミングは、創造的で多様なアイディアを生み出すための発想法です。ブレインストーミングを行う際は、以下を参考にしましょう。

**Point 1　質より量を重視**

最初の段階では、アイディアの数を重視し、できるだけ多くのアイディアを出すことに重点を置きましょう。後で整理や絞り込みを行うことができます。

**Point 2　アイディアの結合**

さまざまなアイディアを組み合わせることで、新たなアイディアが生まれる場合があります。

**Point 3　アイディアの整理と評価**

ブレインストーミングの後に、集まったアイディアを整理し、優先順位をつけることで実現可能性や効果を評価します。

---

| 「自己紹介」をするときの Brainstorming の例 |
|---|

**Greeting and My Name**
Ichiro Suzuki

**Hometown**
Adachi, Tokyo
Senju High School

**Self-Introduction**

**Family**
father, mother, sister
play tennis together

**Class Goals**
want to get more confident
make new friends

# ② Outline (アウトライン)

ブレインストーミングで整理した内容をプレゼンテーションに仕上げるため、アウトラインを作成することは非常に重要です。アウトラインはプレゼンテーションの構造を整理し、ロジカルな流れを確立するのに役立ちます。

......................................................................

### ❶ 導入部の作成 (Introduction)

プレゼンテーションの最初に、自己紹介と話題の導入を行います。ここで聴衆の興味を引き、プレゼンテーション全体のテーマや目的を紹介します。

### ❷ メインアイディアの列挙 (Body)

プレゼンテーションの中核となるメインアイディアを列挙します。これらのアイディアがプレゼンテーションの各セクションとなります。

### ❸ 論理的な順序の確立

メインアイディアを論理的な順序で配置します。情報がスムーズにつながり、聴衆が理解しやすい流れを作ります。時系列、問題と解決策、一般論から具体例へといった、さまざまな論理展開の順序を検討します。

### ❹ 具体的なサポート情報を用意

各メインアイディアをサポートするためのデータ、事例、引用などの具体的な情報を用意します。これにより、話を裏付けて説得力を高めることができます。

### ❺ 段落 (セクション) 間の移行を工夫

段落間の移り変わりをスムーズにするために、段落間の「つながり」を考えます。前の段落と次の段落を繋ぐ言葉やフレーズを使い、聴衆が理解しやすいように工夫します。

### ❻ まとめの作成 (Conclusion)

プレゼンテーションの最後に、まとめや結論を述べるセクションを追加します。聴衆に残すべき印象を形成するために、要点を再強調します。

......................................................................

アウトラインをしっかりと作成することでプレゼンテーションの準備がスムーズに進み、聴衆に効果的に情報を伝えることができます。

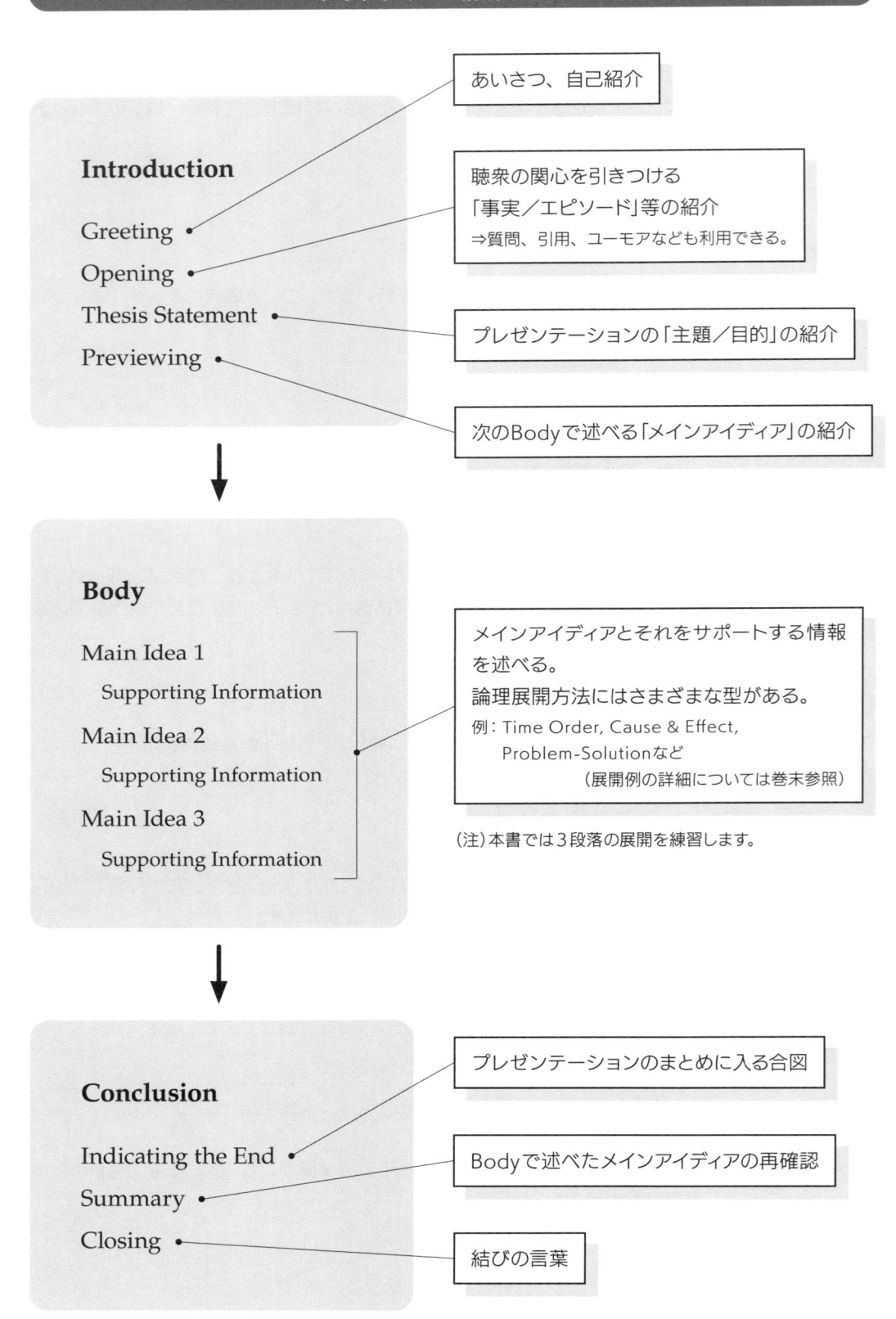

**Introduction**

Greeting — あいさつ、自己紹介

Opening — 聴衆の関心を引きつける「事実／エピソード」等の紹介 ⇒質問、引用、ユーモアなども利用できる。

Thesis Statement — プレゼンテーションの「主題／目的」の紹介

Previewing — 次のBodyで述べる「メインアイディア」の紹介

**Body**

Main Idea 1
    Supporting Information
Main Idea 2
    Supporting Information
Main Idea 3
    Supporting Information

メインアイディアとそれをサポートする情報を述べる。
論理展開方法にはさまざまな型がある。
例：Time Order, Cause & Effect, Problem-Solutionなど
（展開例の詳細については巻末参照）

（注）本書では3段落の展開を練習します。

**Conclusion**

プレゼンテーションのまとめに入る合図

Indicating the End

Summary — Bodyで述べたメインアイディアの再確認

Closing — 結びの言葉

「自己紹介」をするときの Outline の例

## Outline

### I. Introduction

1. Greeting: _Good morning_
2. Opening: _My name is Ichiro Suzuki._
3. Thesis Statement: _Introduce myself_
4. Previewing: _my hometown, my family, and class goals_

↓

### II. Body

1. Main Idea 1

   Hometown: Adachi, Tokyo
   High School: Senju high school

2. Main Idea 2

   Family: father, mother, sister
   Hobby: play tennis with family on weekend

3. Main Idea 3

   Class Goals: want to get more confident in speaking English
   make new friends

↓

### III. Conclusion

1. Indicating the End: _Now you know better about me._
2. Summary: _I hope to know you better too._
3. Closing: _Thank you_

## 3 メモの作成

プレゼンテーションを行う際は原稿を朗読するのではなく、事前にメモを準備し、メモに書かれたキーワードから英文を考え、自分の言葉で伝えられるように努めることが大切です。

| 「自己紹介」をするときのメモの例 |
| --- |

**1**
good morning
name: Ichiro Suzuki
introduce myself
hometown
family; father, mother, sister
class goals: confident, more friends

**2**
hometown
born and raised in Adachi
Senju high school

**3**
family
father
mother
sister
hobby: tennis

**4**
class goals
more confident in speaking English
make new friends

**5**
know about me better
hope to know you
thanks

> 文をすべて書くのではなく、キーワードなどを箇条書きにする

### 各種表現例を利用する

本書には、巻末に論理展開の型ごとに、さまざまな英語の表現例を掲載していますので、英文を考える際に参照するとよいでしょう。これらの表現例を論理的、効果的に組み合わせることで、聴衆の印象に残るプレゼンテーションをすることができます。

「自己紹介」のプレゼンテーションの例

 02

Good morning, everyone. I am delighted to have this opportunity to introduce myself. My name is Ichiro Suzuki, and I would like to share a bit about who I am, where I come from, and what I hope to achieve.

I was born and raised in Adachi, Tokyo. After completing my early education, I had the privilege of attending Senju High School.

I am fortunate to have a loving and supportive family consisting of my father, mother, and sister. Family is incredibly important to me, and we often engage in activities that strengthen our bonds. One of our favorite weekend activities is playing tennis together.

I have set myself some goals for personal and academic growth. In the realm of language, I am determined to become more confident in speaking English. Moreover, I am eager to make new friends during this journey.

In conclusion, I am excited to embrace the future with open arms. Through improving my English and building new friendships, I hope to make the most of this opportunity.

Thank you for your time and attention. I look forward to getting to know every one of you better.

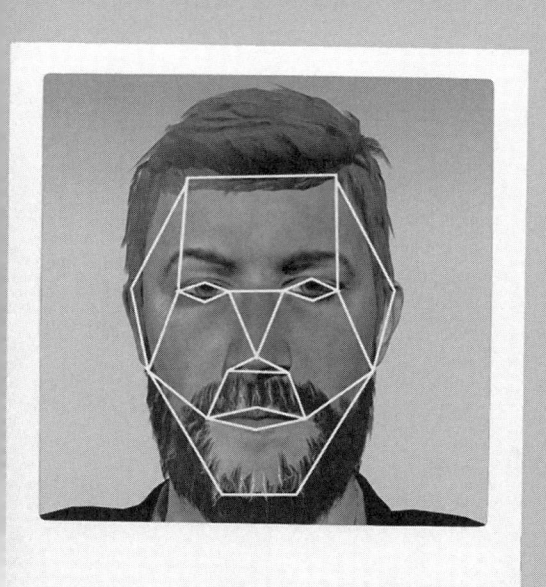

## Facial Recognition: What's in a Face?

**Unit 1**

スマートフォンの顔認証システムを利用していますか。このシステムは、ほかにはどのような場所で利用されているでしょうか。顔認証は便利だと思いますか。問題点は何でしょうか。顔認証システムがどのように使われているか、利便性、問題点などについて調べ、自らの意見を発表しましょう。

# ■ WARM-UP

### 1 OPENING QUESTIONS

*Answer the following questions in English.*

1. When and where is facial recognition technology used?

2. Do you use this technology? Why or why not?

3. What do you think about this technology?

*Match the word with its definition in Japanese.*

1. biometric     _____
2. authenticate     _____
3. trait     _____
4. pupil     _____
5. mundane     _____

a. 特徴
b. ありふれた
c. 瞳孔
d. 生物測定の
e. 本物と証明する

## 3 VOCABULARY PRACTICE

*Fill in the blanks with the most appropriate word from the box below.*

1. Can you provide any proof of _____?
2. The wind turbines are used to _____ electricity.
3. The Constitution protects the _____ of the people.
4. The device gives a greater _____ of safety.
5. It's interesting to _____ these two cars.

> generate    compare    identity    margin    liberty

# Ⅲ▶ LISTENING (Input Information)

## 1 NOTE TAKING

[Time 01:36]    03

*Watch the video, listen to the recording, and fill in the blanks with the most appropriate words.*

### Facial Recognition

1. Definition
   - Biometric technology to identify a(n) 1_____
   - From a 2_____ or a facial image

2. Purposes

   • To authenticate 3_____

   • To check if people are who they 4_____ to be

3. Process

   • Generation of a(n) 5_____ based on the face's unique

     6_____

     e.g., ears, pupils, 7_____, eyebrows,

     8_____, skin grain,

     ✕ hair, 9_____

   • Comparison of the face print with images in

     the 10_____

   • Reducing errors: good 11_____, correct

     12_____

4. Uses

   • Fighting 13_____

   • Accessing bank accounts and 14_____ platforms

5. Concerns

   • Threat to 15_____ and individual liberties

## 2 COMPREHENSION QUESTIONS

*Write T if the statement is true and F if it is false.*

1. Facial recognition is a biometric technology.                                    _____

2. The image is compared to an existing image in a database.                         _____

3. Hair and clothes are taken into consideration.                                    _____

4. The face doesn't have to be a well-lit, full face at a correct distance from
   the lens.                                                                         _____

5. This technology could have a negative impact on privacy and
   individual liberties.                                                             _____

# **III** SPEAKING (Exchange Ideas)

## 1  SPEAKING PRACTICE

 EC CD 04, 05

*There are diverse opinions about the private use of facial recognition technology. Listen to the two dialogs and practice them with your partner. Then think about your own views of facial recognition technology. Which opinion is closer to your own?*

## Facial Recognition Technology for Private Use

| | DIALOG 1 | DIALOG 2 |
|---|---|---|
| Kei | Do you use facial recognition technology on your smartphone? | Do you use facial recognition technology on your smartphone? |
| Emi | Yes, I use it every time I turn it on. It's very convenient. | No, I don't use it. I think it is risky. |
| Kei | Do you have any problem using it? | Why do you think so? |
| Emi | No, not at all. Do you think there are some problems? | It would cause serious problems if my face ID was stolen. |
| Kei | Yes, if my face ID was stolen, it would be a big problem. | Yes, it is as important as a PIN. |
| Emi | I think it is safer and easier than remembering my PIN. | That's what I think, so I do not use it personally. |

## 2  CREATE A DIALOG

*Think about the public use of facial recognition technology based on your own opinions. Complete the following dialog and practice it with your partner.*

## Facial Recognition Technology for Public Use

**You:** Have you been to any event using facial recognition technology to check people at the entrance?

**Your partner:** (Yes / No) _____

**You:** (Where did you go…) _____

**Your partner:** _____

**You:**　　　　　(What do you think…) _____

**Your partner:** _____

# Ⅳ PRESENTATION (Output Your Ideas)

**Argument Points**　The Convenience and Privacy Problems of Facial Recognition Technology

### Process 1　Research

*Search the Internet or use other means to find where facial recognition technologies are being used and think about your own opinions on the subject.*

### Process 2　Brainstorming

*What are some of the advantages and disadvantages of facial recognition technology? In the following diagram, summarize the information you have researched. Add your own ideas as needed.*

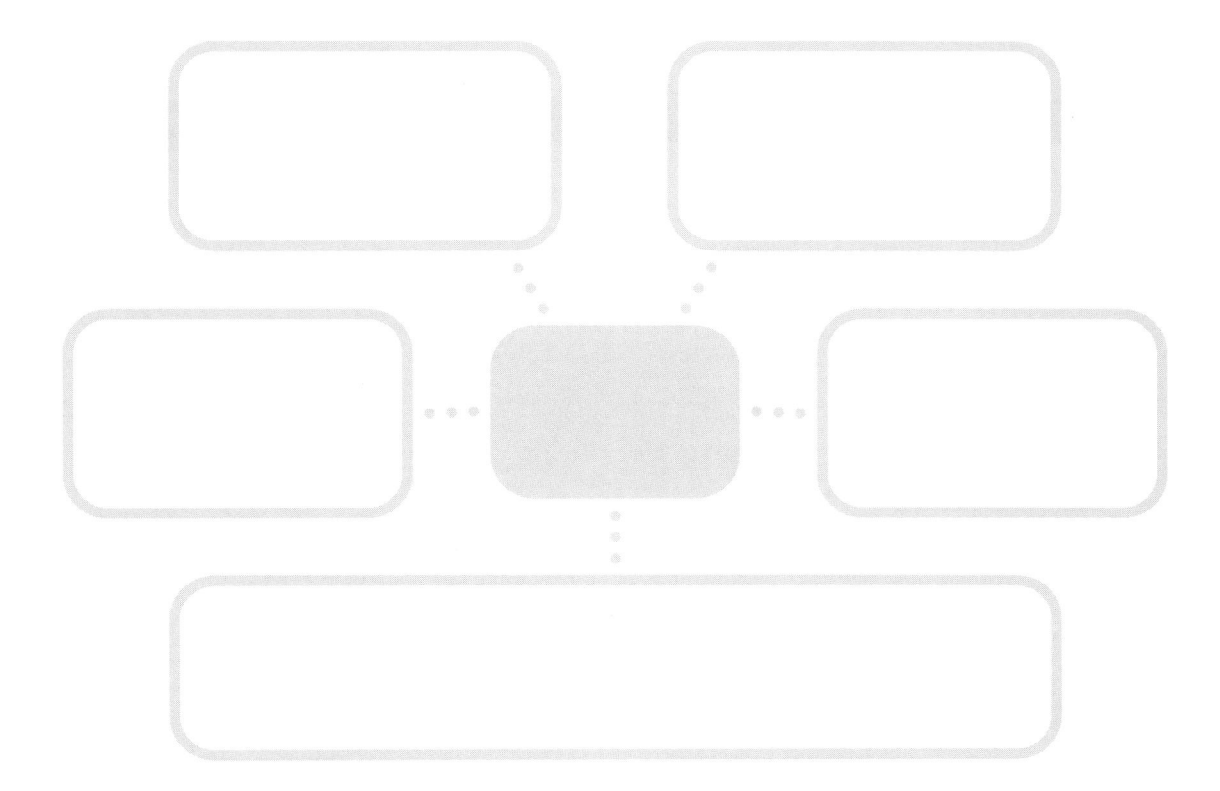

*Summarize what you have researched and the ideas you have come up with in Process 1 and 2 and compose a presentation according to the following outline.*

## Outline

### I. Introduction

**1.** Greeting

_____

**2.** Opening

_____

**3.** Thesis Statement

_____

**4.** Previewing

_____

↓

### II. Body

**1.** Main Idea 1

**2.** Main Idea 2

**3.** Main Idea 3

↓

### III. Conclusion

**1.** Indicating the End

_____

**2.** Summary

_____

**3.** Closing

_____

**Process 4** **Presenting**

*Based on the outline you have created, present it to the entire class.*

# 目的を明確にする

> プレゼンテーションの目的を明確にし、伝えたいことを明確にします。明確な目的を持って話を進めることが重要です。

## ❶研究結果を報告する

研究課題を実施した結果を報告するために、プレゼンテーションを行う場合があります。この場合、目的は研究の結果を詳しく説明することです。

## ❷議論を促す

ディベートや論争に関するテーマについて話をする場合、目的は聴衆の議論を促すことです。この場合、明確に異なる立場を提示することが重要です。

## ❸資料を説明する

プロジェクトや報告書の結果を説明するためにプレゼンテーションを行う場合、目的はその資料を詳しく説明することです。

## ❹スキルを紹介する

自分自身のスキルや経験を紹介するために、プレゼンテーションを行う場合があります。この場合、目的は自分自身のスキルや経験を聴衆に伝えることです。

## ❺問題解決策を提供する

学生が特定の問題に関する解決策を提供するためにプレゼンテーションを行う場合があります。この場合、目的は聴衆に対してその問題の背景や解決策を明確に説明することです。

# Daylight Saving Time

**Unit 2**

Daylight Saving Time (サマータイム) の議論には賛否両論があります。良い点としては、夏時間を利用することで日中の有効利用が促進され、エネルギーの節約や生産性の向上が期待されます。一方で、時刻の変更による生活リズムの乱れや健康への影響が懸念されます。議論は経済効果や生活への影響、環境への影響など多岐にわたります。サマータイムについて考えましょう。

## I ▸ WARM-UP

### 1 OPENING QUESTIONS

*Answer the following questions in English.*

1. What is daylight saving time?

   _____

2. What is the reason for using it?

   _____

3. What are some potential risks?

   _____

## 2 │ VOCABULARY STUDY

*Match the word with its definition in Japanese.*

1. saying     _____
2. negligible     _____
3. unsettle     _____
4. disrupt     _____
5. concept     _____

a. 概念
b. ことわざ
c. 混乱させる
d. 無視してよい
e. 不安にする

## 3 │ VOCABULARY PRACTICE

*Fill in the blanks with the most appropriate word from the box below.*

1. When you write a report, you must _____ the websites you used for information.
2. Animals like chameleons can _____ their colors to blend into their surroundings.
3. The company reports _____ growth in its profits this year.
4. The ideal amount of exercise _____ day may vary from one person to another.
5. Employees are expected to _____ the code of conduct at their company.

> considerable    cite    observe    per    adapt

# II ▶ LISTENING (Input Information)

## 1 │ NOTE TAKING

[Time 01:24]  06

*Watch the video, listen to the recording, and fill in the blanks with the most appropriate words.*

### Daylight Saving Time

"Spring forward, 1 back."

1. **Origin of Daylight Saving Time**
   - Introduced during WWI in 2_____
   - Fully adopted in the late 3_____ century

2. **Purpose and Benefits**
   - Gain an extra hour of 4_____ in summer
   - Shortening the days in 5_____
   - Suggested by Benjamin Franklin in 6_____ for saving
     7_____
   - Considerable 8_____ benefit
   - Saving 9_____

3. **Criticism and Disadvantages**
   - No proven link between benefits and 10_____ change
   - Negligible 11_____ savings
   - Disruptions in 12_____
   - Difficulties for certain groups like the 13_____, sick, and children

## 2 COMPREHENSION QUESTIONS

*Write T if the statement is true and F if it is false.*

1. Europe didn't fully adopt daylight saving time during World War I. _____

2. Benjamin Franklin suggested daylight saving time to save candles in the summer. _____

3. Daylight saving time cannot reduce energy consumption. _____

4. Farmers generally support daylight saving time due to its effects on agricultural activities. _____

5. The elderly, sick, and children, may face difficulties adapting to daylight saving time. _____

# III▶ SPEAKING (Exchange Ideas)

## 1 SPEAKING PRACTICE

 07, 08

*There are diverse opinions about daylight saving time. Listen to the two dialogs and practice them with your partner. Then think about your views on the subject. Which opinion is closer to your own?*

## Pros & Cons of Daylight Saving Time

| | DIALOG 1 | DIALOG 2 |
|---|---|---|
| Kei | Do you know why we change our clocks twice a year? | Do you think it is good to change our clocks twice a year? |
| Emi | Yes, it's called daylight saving time. We do it to have more daylight in the evenings. | Losing and gaining an hour can mess up our sleep. |
| Kei | Right! That way, we can play outside longer after school. | True. Some find it hard getting used to the new time. |
| Emi | Yes, and it saves energy by using sunlight instead of artificial lights. | Yes, especially older people and kids. It takes time to adjust. |
| Kei | I heard it makes roads safer too. There are fewer accidents in daylight. | I heard farmers aren't fans because it messes with their animals' routines. |
| Emi | That's right. Daylight saving time is good for us in lots of ways. | Right. Daylight saving time has its downsides too. |

## 2 CREATE A DIALOG

*Think about introducing daylight saving time in Japan based on your opinions. Complete the following dialog and practice it with your partner.*

### Introduction of Daylight Saving Time in Japan

**You:**          Have you heard about daylight saving time?

**Your partner:** ( Yes / No ), _____

**You:**          Right. _____

**Your partner:** Does Japan implement daylight saving time?

**You:** No, _____

**Your partner:** _____

**You:** _____

# **Ⅳ** PRESENTATION (Output Your Ideas)

**Argument Points** **The Pros and Cons of Daylight Saving Time**

### Process 1 Research

*Search the Internet or use other means to find what the benefits and problems of daylight saving time are and what impact they have on our lives. Then think about your own opinions on the subject.*

### Process 2 Brainstorming

*What are your opinions about the introduction of daylight saving time in Japan? In the following diagram, summarize the information you have researched. Add your own ideas as needed.*

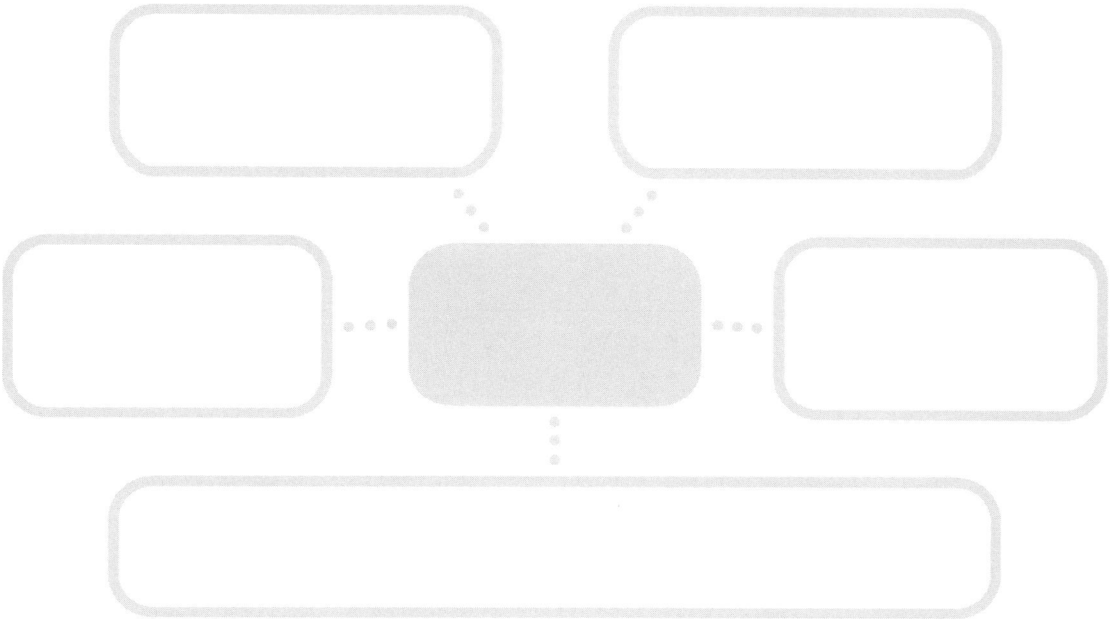

*Summarize what you have researched and the ideas you have come up with in Process 1 and 2 and compose a presentation according to the following outline.*

## Outline

### I. Introduction

**1.** Greeting

_____

**2.** Opening

_____

**3.** Thesis Statement

_____

**4.** Previewing

_____

↓

### II. Body

**1.** Main Idea 1

_____

**2.** Main Idea 2

_____

**3.** Main Idea 3

↓

### III. Conclusion

**1.** Indicating the End

_____

**2.** Summary

_____

**3.** Closing

_____

**Process 4**  **Presenting**

*Based on the outline you have created, present it to the entire class.*

# 対象者を考慮する

> プレゼンテーションをする対象者を考慮し、適切な言葉や表現を選びます。

### ❶聴衆の年齢層を考慮する

聴衆の年齢層に応じて、プレゼンテーションのスタイルや言葉遣い、使用する用語など
を調整することが重要です。

### ❷聴衆の知識レベルを考慮する

聴衆の知識レベルに応じて、プレゼンテーションの内容や説明の深さを調整することが
重要です。

### ❸聴衆の背景を考慮する

聴衆の背景に応じて、プレゼンテーションの例や比喩、使用する言葉を調整することが
重要です。

### ❹聴衆の関心を考慮する

聴衆の関心に応じて、プレゼンテーションの内容やスタイルを調整することが重要です。

### ❺聴衆の文化的背景を考慮する

聴衆の文化的背景に応じて、プレゼンテーションのスタイルや内容、使用する例や比喩
などを調整することが重要です。

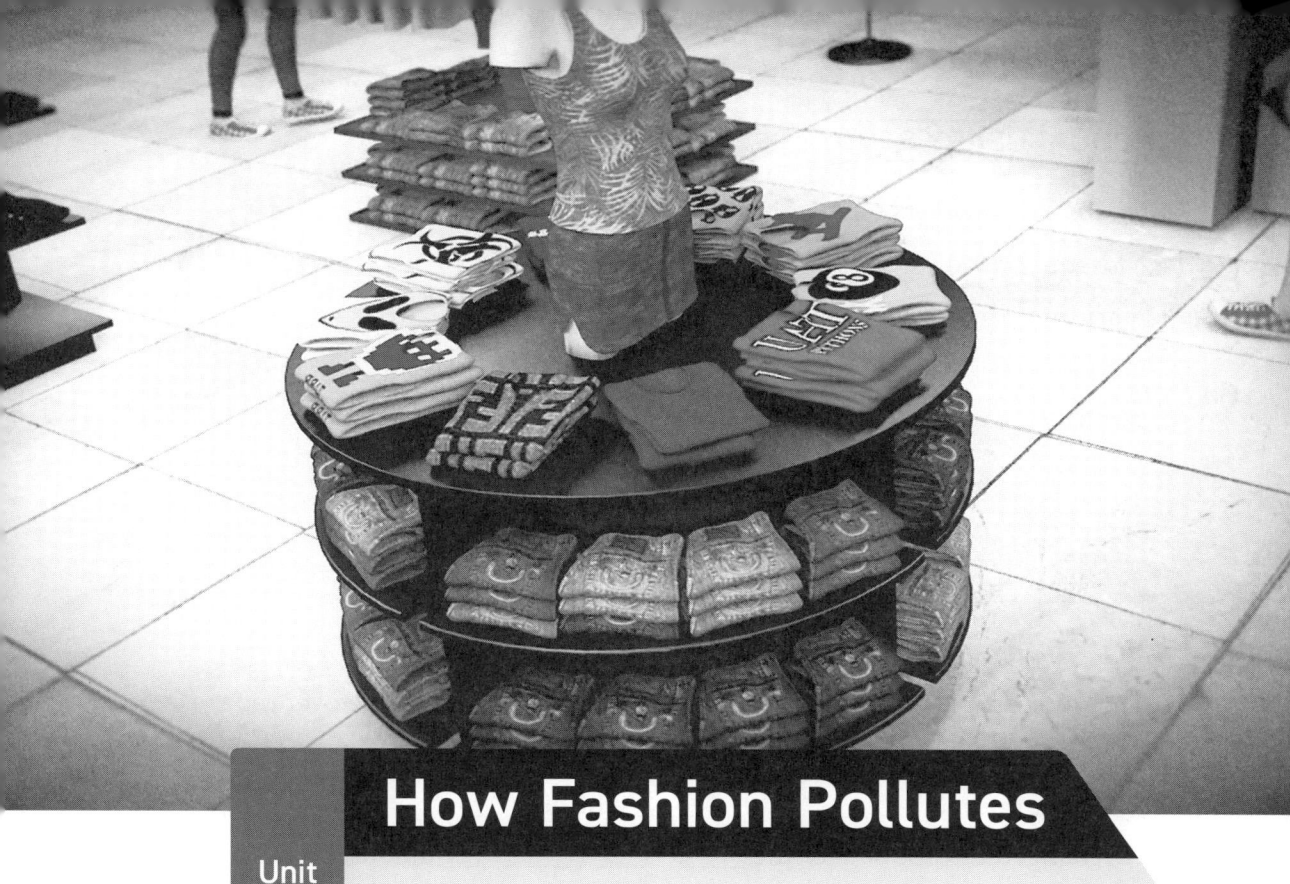

# How Fashion Pollutes

**Unit 3**

ファッションに興味はありますか。どこで衣類を購入しますか。ファストファッションは好きですか。衣類の原料の作成、製造、輸送、洗濯などで環境への影響が懸念されていることを考えたことがありますか。環境にやさしい衣類とはどのようなものでしょうか。

# ▶ WARM-UP

## 1 OPENING QUESTIONS

*Answer the following questions in English.*

1. When and where do you usually buy new clothes?

   _____

2. What kind of fashion style do you like and why?

   _____

3. What do you think is the connection between fashion and pollution?

   _____

## 2 VOCABULARY STUDY

*Match the word with its definition in Japanese.*

1. consequence _____
2. maritime _____
3. footprint _____
4. pesticide _____
5. textile _____

a. 天然資源の消費量
b. 布地、織物
c. 海の
d. 結果
e. 殺虫剤

## 3 VOCABULARY PRACTICE

*Fill in the blanks with the most appropriate word from the box below.*

1. The color purple may be made by _____ blue over red.
2. The application of _____ increased the size of the plants.
3. Bicycling doesn't _____ the air.
4. He changed his pounds for the _____ amount in dollars.
5. The fire caused _____ damage to the church.

> pollute   considerable   fertilizer   dyeing   equivalent

# II▶ LISTENING (Input Information)

## 1 NOTE TAKING

[Time 01:36]  EC DVD CD 09

*Watch the video, listen to the recording, and fill in the blanks with the most appropriate words.*

### How Fashion Pollutes

1. Clothing
   - 1 _____ items sold per year
   - Twice more than 15 years ago
   - Consequence of 2 _____

2. Materials

- 3 _____%: cotton

  problems: use of 4 _____, 5 _____,

  6 _____

- 60%: 7 _____

  problem: 8 _____

3. Use of Dangerous Products

- 9 _____

- 10 _____ out

- 11 _____ the raw material

4. Transportation

5. Washing

- 12 _____ released into the oceans

- 13 _____ tons per year

- the equivalent of 14 _____ bottles of plastic

6. Greenhouse Gases

- 15 _____ tons

## 2 | COMPREHENSION QUESTIONS

*Write T if the statement is true and F if it is false.*

1. As a result of fast fashion popularity, clothing sales have doubled in 15 years. _____

2. Making clothes from cotton requires a lot of water. _____

3. Clothes may not cause pollution in homes. _____

4. Washing polyester shirts and shorts releases 5,000 tons of micro-fibers per year. _____

5. Textiles release more greenhouse gases than international air travel and maritime shipping combined. _____

# ▐▐▐▶ SPEAKING (Exchange Ideas)

## 1 SPEAKING PRACTICE

 10, 11

*There are diverse opinions about fashion preferences. Listen to the two dialogs and practice them with your partner. Then think about your own preference for fashion. Which opinion is closer to your own?*

## Fashion: Fast vs Luxury

| | DIALOG 1 | DIALOG 2 |
|---|---|---|
| Kei | Which fashion do you usually prefer to buy, fast or luxury? | Which fashion do you usually prefer to buy, fast or luxury? |
| Emi | I prefer buying fast fashion items. | I usually prefer buying luxury fashion items. |
| Kei | Why is that? | Why is that? |
| Emi | It is very cheap, and I can buy many items without spending too much money. | It is rather expensive, but these items usually last longer, and I can wear them for a long time. |
| Kei | Don't you think it is a waste of money if you buy clothes again and again? | Yeah, but not many people can afford to buy luxury items. |
| Emi | Well, fashion changes every year, and I can follow the latest trends. | That is one of the advantages. I don't see many people wearing the same clothes when I go out. |

## 2 CREATE A DIALOG

*Think about the materials used for clothing based on your own opinions. Complete the following dialog and practice it with your partner.*

## Clothing Materials

**You:**  What kind of materials do you usually prefer for your clothing?

**Your partner:** (natural/synthetic) _____

| You: | (Why do you prefer…) _____ |
|------|---------------------------------------------------|
| **Your partner:** | _____ |
| You: | (What do you think…) _____ |
| **Your partner:** | _____ |

# Ⅳ PRESENTATION (Output Your Ideas)

**Argument Points** ⟩ **The Problems of Fast Fashion and Its Effect on the Environment**

### Process 1   Research

*Search the Internet or use other methods to discover the environmental problems caused by fast fashion and ways to be fashionable while also conserving the environment. Then think about your own opinions of fast fashion.*

### Process 2   Brainstorming

*What are some of the advantages and disadvantages of fast fashion? In the following diagram, summarize the information you have researched. Add your own ideas as needed.*

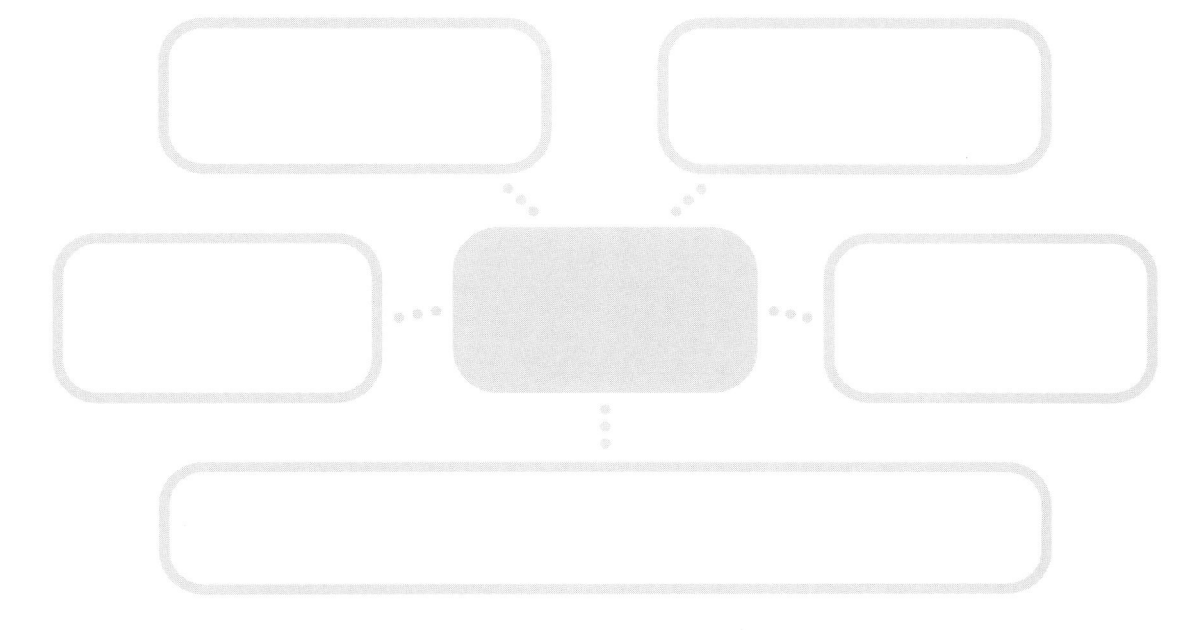

*Summarize what you have researched and the ideas you have come up with in Process 1 and 2 and compose a presentation according to the following outline.*

## Outline

### I. Introduction

**1.** Greeting

**2.** Opening

**3.** Thesis Statement

**4.** Previewing

↓

### II. Body

**1.** Main Idea 1

**2.** Main Idea 2

**3.** Main Idea 3

↓

## III. Conclusion

**1.** Indicating the End

_____

**2.** Summary

_____

**3.** Closing

_____

**Process 4** **Presenting**

*Based on the outline you have created, present it to the entire class.*

# 構造化されたプレゼンテーションを作成する

> プレゼンテーションを作成する前に、どのような構造にするか選択します。

## ❶問題解決型プレゼンテーション

プレゼンテーションの最初に、問題点を明確にし、その問題を解決するための解決策を提案するようなプレゼンテーションの構造を取ることができます。

## ❷比較型プレゼンテーション

競合するものとの比較を行うプレゼンテーションの場合、自らの提案の優位性を訴求することが大切です。自らの強みを明確にし、競合するものとの差別化ポイントを示すようなプレゼンテーションの構造を取ることができます。

## ❸階層型プレゼンテーション

プレゼンテーションの大まかな流れを、章立てにした形で説明することができます。階層型プレゼンテーションは、論理的な流れを持たせることができ、聴衆にわかりやすいプレゼンテーションになります。

## ❹経験談型プレゼンテーション

自身が体験したことを通じて、知識や教訓を共有するプレゼンテーションの構造を取ることができます。自分自身が経験した出来事を交えながら、プレゼンテーションを進めることで、聴衆に強い印象を残すことができます。

## ❺プロセス型プレゼンテーション

作業工程など、特定のプロセスを説明するプレゼンテーションの場合、段階を追って説明する構造を取ることができます。段階的に進めることで、聴衆に理解しやすく、全体像を把握することができるようなプレゼンテーションになります。

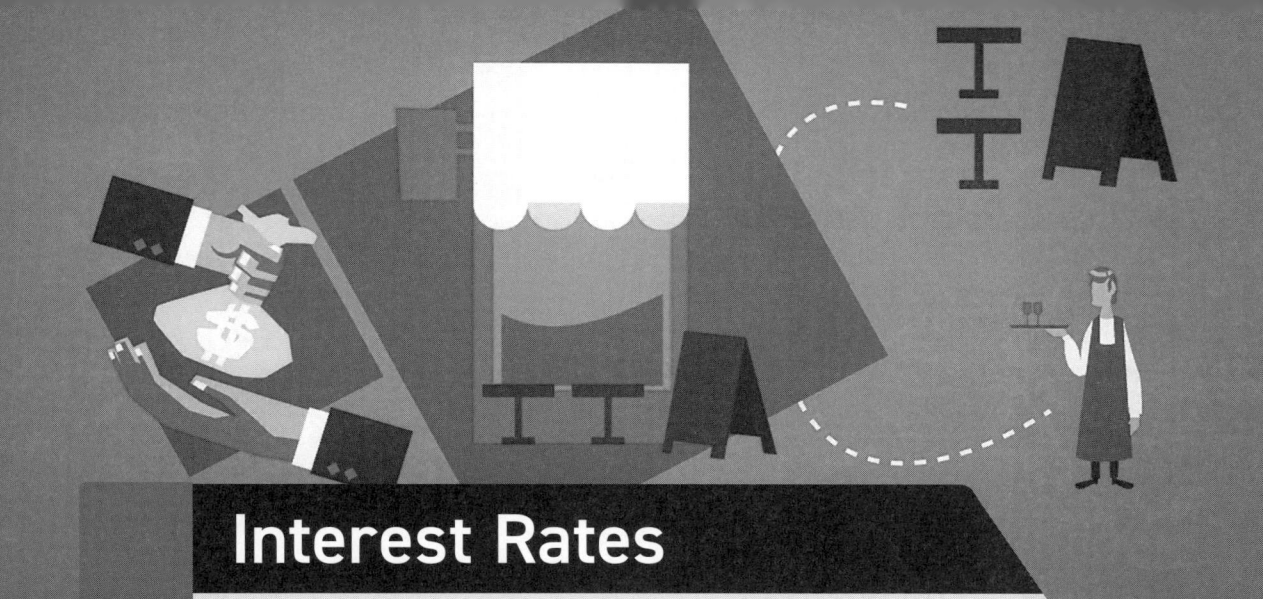

# Interest Rates

金利政策は、中央銀行が金利を調整することで経済全体の動向を制御する重要な政策手段です。この政策は、経済の状況に応じて、金利を引き上げたり引き下げたりすることで、消費、投資、インフレ、そして為替レートなどに直接的な影響を与える役割を果たします。金利を引き上げると、貯蓄が増えて消費が抑制されることで物価上昇を抑える効果がありますが、その一方で企業の投資意欲が減少し、景気が低迷するリスクも生じます。一方、金利を下げると、企業の投資や個人の消費が促進され、景気が活性化する可能性がありますが、その結果としてインフレが進行し、物価が不安定になるリスクが高まります。このように、金利政策は、経済のバランスを保ちながら成長を促すために重要な役割を担っており、その効果や影響について慎重に考える必要があります。金利政策について、さらに深く考えてみましょう。

**Unit 4**

## ▶ WARM-UP

### 1 OPENING QUESTIONS

*Answer the following questions in English.*

1. What do you know about interest rates?

2. How do they influence borrowing and saving?

3. What are the potential consequences of prolonged low interest rates?

*Match the word with its definition in Japanese.*

1. lender _____
2. splash out on _____
3. retailer _____
4. intervene _____
5. mortgage _____

a. 抵当、担保
b. 小売業者
c. 貸し手
d. 介在する
e. 〜にお金を派手に使う

## 3 VOCABULARY PRACTICE

*Fill in the blanks with the most appropriate word from the box below.*

1. The teacher provided a _____ to help students organize their essays.

2. Prices are going up because of _____.

3. The dollar is the _____ used in the United States.

4. Exercise can _____ your energy levels.

5. The factory uses _____ to make cars.

> boost    framework    machinery    currency    inflation

# II▶ LISTENING (Input Information)

## 1 NOTE TAKING

[Time 02:11]   12

*Watch the video, listen to the recording, and fill in the blanks with the most appropriate words.*

### Understanding Interest Rates and Their Impact

1. Interest Rate

   • The cost of 1_____ money or the reward for

   2_____

- The base rate: set by the 3_____ bank
- Central banks > 4_____ banks > businesses and individuals
- Loans for promoting 5_____

2. **Effects of Lower Base Rate**

- Businesses: more likely to 6_____ money for investment
- Individuals: more likely to get a loan for 7_____ or
  8_____
- To boost a sluggish economy: 9_____ interest rate

3. **Impact of Interest Rate Changes**

- Main task of the central bank: sustainable growth of
  10_____
- Intervention for rapid inflation: 11_____ interest rates
- Individuals: more likely to 12_____ money
- Companies: less likely to invest in 13_____
- Retailers: more likely to lower prices to encourage
  14_____

4. **Overall Impact**

- Interest rates: affect 15_____ people

---

**2 COMPREHENSION QUESTIONS**

*Write T if the statement is true and F if it is false.*

1. Interest is the cost of borrowing money or the reward for saving. _____

2. The base rate set by a country's central bank doesn't impact the economy. _____

3. Central banks do not charge interest on loans to commercial banks. _____

4. Lowering the base rate makes saving more attractive. _____

5. Introducing a negative interest rate can encourage lenders to invest in the real economy. _____

# **III** SPEAKING (Exchange Ideas)

**1 SPEAKING PRACTICE**

 EC CD 13, 14

*There are diverse opinions about interest rates. Listen to the two dialogs and practice them with your partner. Then think about your opinions on the subject. Which opinion is closer to your own?*

## Interest Rates and Their Economic Impact

|  | DIALOG 1 | DIALOG 2 |
|---|---|---|
| Kei | Do you know what interest rates are? | Have you heard about how interest rates affect the economy? |
| Emi | Yes, interest is the money we pay when we borrow from the bank, right? | Yes, I think it's harder to borrow money when interest rates are high. |
| Kei | Exactly. And when interest rates go down, is it better to save or spend? | That's correct. And what happens when borrowing becomes harder? |
| Emi | I think it's better to spend because borrowing is cheaper. | People and businesses spend less, and the economy slows down. |
| Kei | That's right. Lower interest rates make people spend more and help the economy. | Exactly. So, interest rates play a big role in how our economy grows or slows down. |
| Emi | Yes, lower interest rates make borrowing cheaper, so people spend more. | Absolutely. Interest rates have a big impact on economic activity. |

**2 CREATE A DIALOG**

*Think about interest rates based on your own opinions. Complete the following dialog and practice it with your partner.*

## Problems of Low Interest Rate

**You:** Have you heard about the current low interest rates?

**Your partner:** Yes, _____

You: _____

Your partner: _____

You: _____

Your partner: _____

You: _____

# **IV** PRESENTATION (Output Your Ideas)

**Argument Points**   The Pros and Cons of Interest Rates

### Process 1   Research

*Search the Internet or use other means to find about interest rates, and the impact they have on our lives when they are low or high. Then think about your own opinions on the subject.*

### Process 2   Brainstorming

*What are your opinions about interest rates? In the following diagram, summarize the information you have researched. Add your own ideas as needed.*

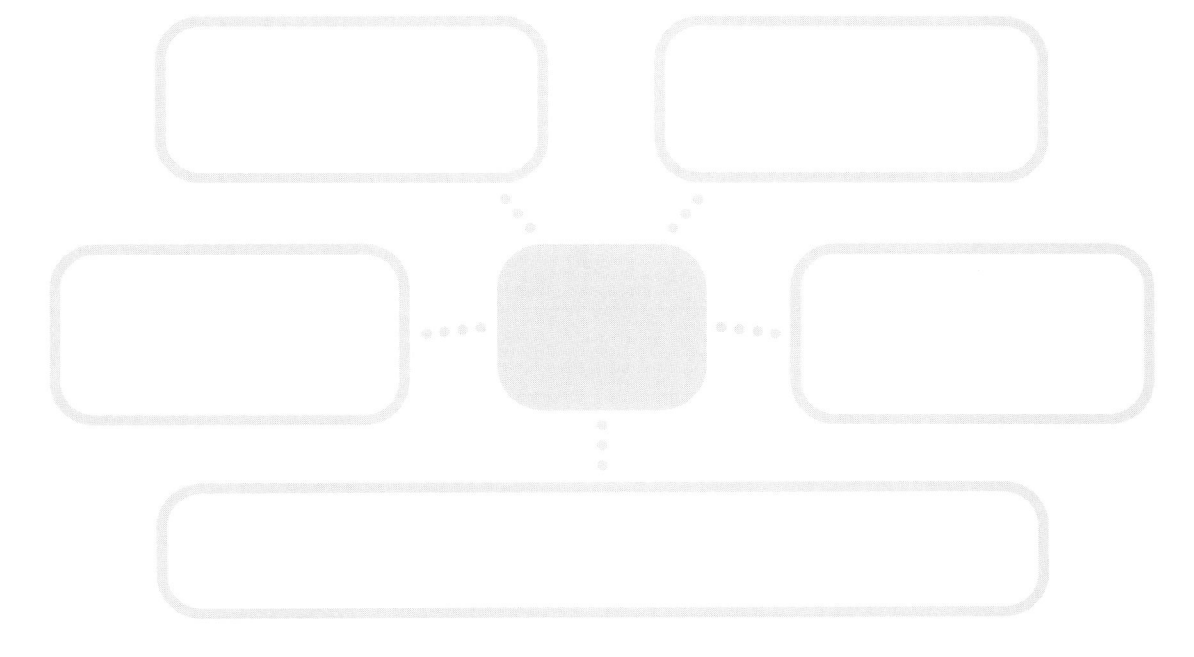

*Summarize what you have researched and the ideas you have come up with in Process 1 and 2 and compose a presentation according to the following outline.*

## Outline

### I. Introduction

1. Greeting

   _____

2. Opening

   _____

3. Thesis Statement

   _____

4. Previewing

   _____

↓

### II. Body

1. Main Idea 1

   ┌─────────────────────────────────────────┐
   │                                         │
   │                                         │
   │                                         │
   │                                         │
   └─────────────────────────────────────────┘

2. Main Idea 2

   ┌─────────────────────────────────────────┐
   │                                         │
   │                                         │
   │                                         │
   │                                         │
   └─────────────────────────────────────────┘

3. Main Idea 3

<br><br><br><br>

↓

**III. Conclusion**

1. Indicating the End

_____

2. Summary

_____

3. Closing

_____

**Process 4  Presenting**

*Based on the outline you have created, present it to the entire class.*

# タイムマネジメントを考慮する

時間内にプレゼンテーションを終えるように、タイムマネジメントを考慮します。

## ❶時間配分を事前に決める

プレゼンテーションの全体時間や、各パートの時間配分を事前に決めることで、プレゼンテーション中に時間がオーバーすることを避けることができます。

## ❷スライド数に応じた時間配分を考える

プレゼンテーションのスライド数に応じて、スライドごとに割り当てられる時間を考えることで、時間配分を細かく調整することができます。

## ❸練習する

プレゼンテーションを実際に練習することで、全体の時間配分や各パートの時間配分を把握し、実際のプレゼンテーションで時間配分を守ることができます。

## ❹時間を確認する

プレゼンテーション中に時間を確認することで、予定時間内にプレゼンテーションを終えることができます。時計やストップウォッチを準備し、途中で時間を確認するようにしましょう。

## ❺質疑応答に時間を割く

プレゼンテーション中に質問や疑問が出ることがありますが、その質疑応答に時間を割くことができるよう、プレゼンテーションの時間配分に余裕を持たせるようにしましょう。質問に答えることで、聴衆とのコミュニケーションを図ることができます。

# Artificial Intelligence

**Unit 5**

人工知能（AI）は、機械やコンピューターに人間の学習や意思決定などのプロセスを再現させる科学です。最近の技術革新により、AIは急速に進化し、日常生活に浸透しています。AIは、効率的な世界を約束し、ロボットが介護をしたり、冷蔵庫を補充したり、人間の代わりに危険な仕事を行います。しかし、ロボットがほぼすべてのことを行うようになると、数百万の仕事が脅かされる可能性があります。

# ▶ WARM-UP

## 1 OPENING QUESTIONS

*Answer the following questions in English.*

1. What do you know about artificial intelligence?

   _____

2. Do you use artificial intelligence? Why or why not?

   _____

3. What can you do to improve your skills at using artificial intelligence?

   _____

*Match the word or phrase with its definition in Japanese.*

1. mastery         _____
2. in the blink of an eye   _____
3. creep          _____
4. stride         _____
5. manipulate      _____

a. 進歩
b. 忍び寄る
c. 瞬時に
d. 操作する
e. 熟達

## 3  VOCABULARY PRACTICE

*Fill in the blanks with the most appropriate word from the box below.*

1. The doctor used special tools to _____ the problem.
2. They went on a _____ to find the missing treasure.
3. The chef will _____ the recipe perfectly.
4. It is very _____ to play with sharp objects.
5. The project is progressing _____ and will be completed on schedule.

execute   steadily   diagnose   hazardous   quest

# II▶ LISTENING (Input Information)

## 1  NOTE TAKING

[Time 02:21]  WEB動画  EC  DVD  CD  15

*Watch the video, listen to the recording, and fill in the blanks with the most appropriate words.*

### Exploring Artificial Intelligence (AI)

1. Definition of AI

   • Science of programming computers to replicate 1_____ processes

   • 2_____ and decision-making

2. Technological Advances in AI

- Intelligent algorithms

- 3_____ decision-making

3. Examples of AI in Daily Life

- 4_____: become more intelligent

- Cyber assistants: quickly find 5_____

- Autonomous vehicles: improve 6_____ safety

4. Promises of AI

- Highly-7_____ world

- 8_____: handle various tasks

5. Game Playing

- A good measure of 9_____

  e.g., 10_____ and Go

6. AI in Medicine

- 11_____ of illnesses

- As effectively as human 12_____

7. Challenges and Concerns

- Coping with the 13_____ Industrial Revolution

- Challenges for 14_____ and policymakers

- Millions of 15_____ at risk

## 2 COMPREHENSION QUESTIONS

*Write T if the statement is true and F if it is false.*

1. AI means teaching machines to copy humans. _____

2. New technology hasn't significantly changed AI. _____

3. Self-driving cars might cut traffic accidents. _____

4. AI suggests that robots can perform risky jobs. _____

5. The speaker doesn't talk about smart machines harming us. _____

# ▶ SPEAKING (Exchange Ideas)

*There are diverse opinions about Artificial Intelligence. Listen to the two dialogs and practice them with your partner. Then think about your own views about Artificial Intelligence. Which opinion is closer to your own?*

## Pros & Cons of Artificial Intelligence

|  | DIALOG 1 | DIALOG 2 |
|---|---|---|
| **Kei** | AI has changed many industries a lot. | Some people worry about AI. |
| **Emi** | Yes, it makes things work better and faster. | Yes, they're concerned about losing jobs to machines. |
| **Kei** | AI also helps by providing smart decisions from data. | AI also makes people think about privacy and safety. |
| **Emi** | Yes, it can handle lots of data quickly. | That's true. It can gather personal information and analyze it. |
| **Kei** | AI can also do boring work, and saves time. | Some are scared AI might get too smart. |
| **Emi** | That means people can do cooler stuff instead. | Yes, using AI responsibly is important in solving these problems. |

## 2 | CREATE A DIALOG

*Think about the threat of AI to humans based on your own understanding. Complete the following dialog and then practice it with your partner.*

## AI's Threat to Humans

**You:** Have you heard about the concerns regarding AI's threat to humans?

**Your partner:** ( Yes / No ), _____

**You:** (What if AI could outsmart humans?)

**Your partner:** _____

**You:**         (e.g., questions about the ethical use…)

**Your partner:** _____

## Ⅳ PRESENTATION (Output Your Ideas)

**Argument Points** ⟩ **The Pros and Cons of Artificial Intelligence**

### Process 1 | Research

*Search the Internet or use other means to find what the benefits and problems of artificial intelligence are, and what impact they have on our lives. Then think about your own opinions concerning the advancement of artificial intelligence.*

### Process 2 | Brainstorming

*What are your opinions about artificial intelligence? In the following diagram, summarize the information you have researched. Add your own ideas as needed.*

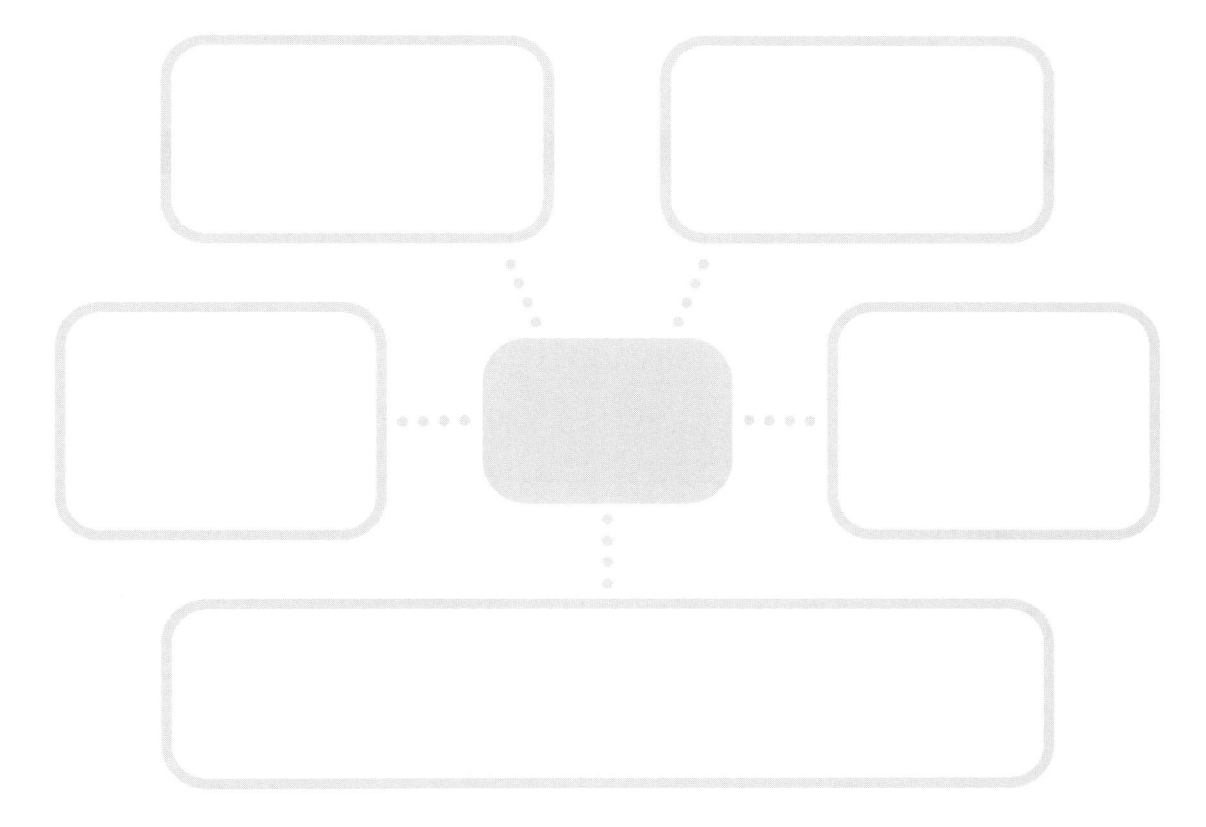

*Summarize what you have researched and the ideas you have come up with in Process 1 and 2 and compose a presentation according to the following outline.*

## Outline

### I. Introduction

**1.** Greeting

**2.** Opening

**3.** Thesis Statement

**4.** Previewing

### II. Body

**1.** Main Idea 1

**2.** Main Idea 2

**3.** Main Idea 3

↓

### III. Conclusion

**1.** Indicating the End

**2.** Summary

**3.** Closing

Process 4    Presenting

*Based on the outline you have created, present it to the entire class.*

# ポイントを強調する

重要なポイントを強調し、視聴者に印象づけます。効果的なポイントの強調は重要です。

### ❶ビジュアルを使った強調

ポイントを視覚的に示すために、スライドやグラフィックを使用します。目立つ色や大きな文字、図表などを使ってポイントを強調し、聴衆の注意を引きます。

### ❷強調表示や太字を活用する

テキストやキーワードを強調表示や太字にすることで、重要なポイントを視覚的に強調します。そのポイントを聴衆に強く印象づけることができます。

### ❸口頭でのリピート

重要なポイントを強調するために、口頭で繰り返し説明します。繰り返し聴衆に伝えることで、ポイントが明確になり、理解度が高まります。

### ❹具体的な例やエピソードを使用する

重要なポイントを具体的な例やエピソードで補強することで、ポイントがより鮮明になります。具体的な事例や体験談を通じて、ポイントをより説得力のあるものにします。

### ❺パラグラフの先頭や終わりに配置する

ポイントを強調するために、パラグラフの先頭や終わりに配置します。これにより、聴衆の関心を引き付け、情報の受け取りやすさを高めます。

# World Heritage Sites

世界遺産は、文化や自然の貴重な遺産を保護し、世界中の人々がその価値を理解し、尊重することを促進する役割を果たしています。これらの遺産は、歴史的な建造物や自然の景観、独自の生態系など、未来の世代に引き継ぐべき重要な財産です。しかし、世界遺産にはいくつかの問題も存在します。例えば、観光客が多く訪れることで遺産に過剰な負荷がかかり、環境への影響が深刻化する場合やまた、保護のための十分な資金や人手が確保されていないことも課題です。これらの問題を解決するためには、持続可能な観光の促進や、地域社会との協力が必要です。世界遺産に関するこれらの問題について、さらに深く考え、発表しましょう。

# ▶ WARM-UP

## 1 OPENING QUESTIONS

*Answer the following questions in English.*

1. Name some of the World Heritage sites you know.

2. Why are World Heritage sites important?

3. What is the purpose of designating places as World Heritage sites?

## 2 VOCABULARY STUDY

*Match the word with its definition in Japanese.*

1. urbanization  _____
2. accordance  _____
3. adhere  _____
4. conflict  _____
5. extinction  _____

a. 準拠
b. 衝突
c. 絶滅
d. 都市化
e. 支持する

## 3 VOCABULARY PRACTICE

*Fill in the blanks with the most appropriate word from the box below.*

1. The team worked in _____ to complete the project on time.
2. It's important to _____ different types of data for analysis.
3. Your _____ is what makes you unique and special.
4. Most countries decided to join the _____ on renewable energy.
5. The organization was _____ to promote environmental conservation.

> collaboration    categorize    identity    convention    founded

# ▐▶ LISTENING (Input Information)

## 1 NOTE TAKING

[Time 01:42]    18

*Watch the video, listen to the recording, and fill in the blanks with the most appropriate words.*

### UNESCO World Heritage Sites

1. UNESCO World Heritage Sites
   - Total: Close to 1_____ sites
   - Cultural sites: Around 2_____

- Natural sites: Over 3_____
- Mixed sites: Around 4_____

2. UNESCO's Establishment
   - Founded in 5_____
   - Headquarters: 6_____

3. UNESCO's Goals
   - Promote collaboration in 7_____, science, and culture
   - Contribute to 8_____ and security

4. World Heritage Convention (1972)
   - Basis for categorizing 9_____ places
   - Encourages international cooperation to 10_____ heritage

5. Threats
   - Natural disasters, pollution, poaching, 11_____
   - Unrestrained 12_____, conflicts, and wars.
   - Several sites on the List of World Heritage in 13_____

6. Protection of Intangible Cultural Heritage
   - UNESCO in 2003
   - 14_____, music, oral traditions, craft skills
   - For protecting cultural 15_____ and traditions

## 2 COMPREHENSION QUESTIONS

*Write T if the statement is true and F if it is false.*

1. There are close to 1,200 UNESCO World Heritage sites worldwide. \_\_\_\_\_

2. UNESCO was founded in 1945. \_\_\_\_\_

3. UNESCO designates only natural heritage sites. \_\_\_\_\_

4. Natural disasters are not a threat to UNESCO World Heritage sites. \_\_\_\_\_

5. A convention to safeguard Intangible Cultural Heritage was adopted by UNESCO in 1972. \_\_\_\_\_

# ▐▐▌ SPEAKING (Exchange Ideas)

## 1 SPEAKING PRACTICE

  19, 20

*There are diverse opinions about the pros and cons of UNESCO World Heritage sites.*
*Listen to the two dialogs and practice them with your partner. Then think about your*
*own views about World Heritage sites. Which opinion is closer to your own?*

## World Heritage Sites

| | DIALOG 1 | | DIALOG 2 |
|---|---|---|---|
| Kei | Do you know about UNESCO World Heritage sites? | | What do you think about UNESCO World Heritage sites? |
| Emi | Yes, they're amazing places known for their cultural or natural importance. | | Well, they do a lot of good, but there are some drawbacks too. |
| Kei | Exactly! They help preserve our heritage for future generations to enjoy. | | Like what? |
| Emi | And they promote international cooperation and understanding. | | Sometimes, too much tourism can damage these sites. |
| Kei | It's great that UNESCO works to protect these valuable sites. | | I see. And there can be conflicts over how to manage and preserve them. |
| Emi | Yes, I would like to visit one of them some time. | | Yes, finding a balance between preservation and accessibility is challenging. |

## 2 CREATE A DIALOG

*Think about World Heritage sites based on your own opinions. Complete the following*
*dialog and practice it with your partner.*

## World Heritage Sites

**You:**        Have you thought about which UNESCO World Heritage site to visit?

**Your partner:** _____

You: _____

Your partner: _____

You: _____

Your partner: _____

You: _____

# Ⅳ PRESENTATION (Output Your Ideas)

**Argument Points** The Pros and Cons of World Heritage Sites

**Process 1  Research**

*Search the Internet or use other means to find the pros and cons of World Heritage sites. Then think about your own opinions on the subject.*

**Process 2  Brainstorming**

*What are your opinions about World Heritage sites? In the following diagram, summarize the information you have researched. Add your own ideas as needed.*

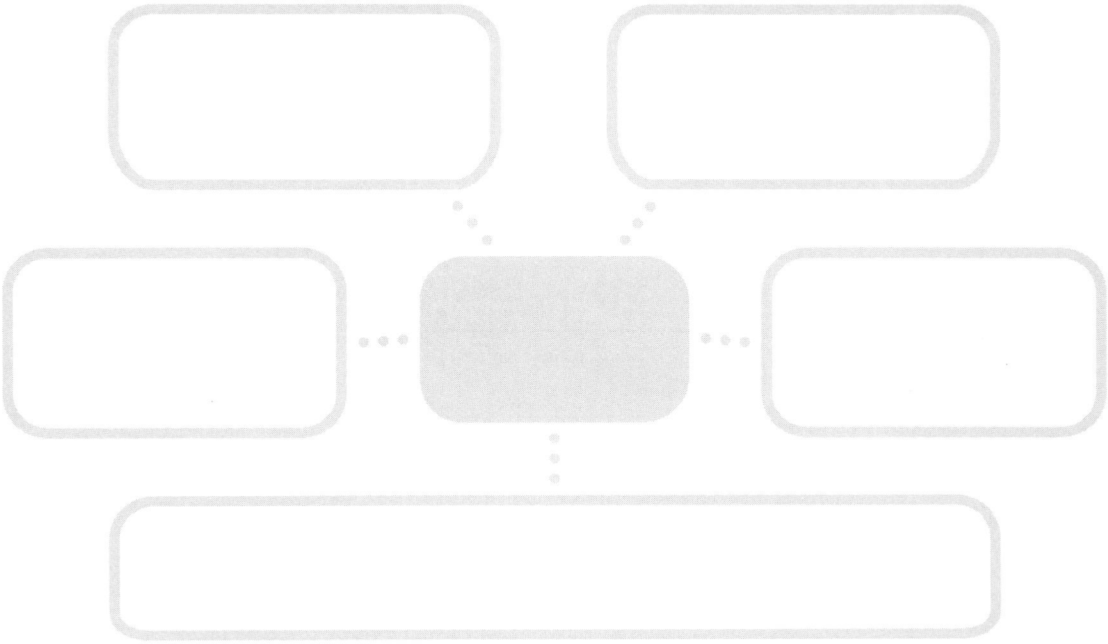

*Summarize what you have researched and the ideas you have come up with in Process 1 and 2 and compose a presentation according to the following outline.*

## Outline

### I. Introduction

**1.** Greeting

_____

**2.** Opening

_____

**3.** Thesis Statement

_____

**4.** Previewing

_____

↓

### II. Body

**1.** Main Idea 1

_____

**2.** Main Idea 2

_____

**3.** Main Idea 3

↓

## III. Conclusion

**1.** Indicating the End

**2.** Summary

**3.** Closing

Process 4　Presenting

*Based on the outline you have created, present it to the entire class.*

# 質疑応答の準備をする

質疑応答に備えて、事前に答えられる質問を予想し、準備をします。

## ❶ 仮想的な質問を予測する

プレゼンテーション中に聴衆が質問する可能性があるトピックを予測し、それに備えて準備します。

## ❷ 質問に対する答えを明確にする

質問に対する答えを明確にするために、情報やデータを整理し、その答えを説明する方法を考えます。また、答えを支持する資料やグラフィックを用意することも大切です。

## ❸ 時間配分を考慮する

プレゼンテーションの時間配分を考慮して、質問に対する答えを簡潔にまとめる方法を検討します。プレゼンテーションの最後に、余った時間を使って聴衆からの質問に答えることもできます。

## ❹ 相手の立場に立って考える

質問に答える前に相手の立場に立って考えることが重要です。聴衆が何を知りたがっているかを理解し、その情報に基づいて答えを調整することが必要です。

## ❺ 練習を行う

質疑応答に備えて、練習を行うことが大切です。クラスメイトや先生にプレゼンテーションを行い、質問に答える練習をすることで、自信をつけることができます。

# Microplastic Pollution

Unit
7

マイクロプラスチックは、環境中に存在する直径5mm以下の微細なプラスチック粒です。最大の発生原因は環境中に投機されたレジ袋やペットボトルを含むプラスチック製品で、紫外線劣化などにより破砕されたものが、河川や下水を経て最終的に海洋に集積します。マイクロプラスチックを削減するためにはどうしたらよいでしょうか。

## ▮▶ WARM-UP

### 1 OPENING QUESTIONS

*Answer the following questions in English.*

1. What do you know about microplastic pollution?

_____

2. Do you use reusable shopping bags? Why or why not?

_____

3. What do you think you can do to reduce microplastics?

_____

## 2　VOCABULARY STUDY

*Match the word with its definition in Japanese.*

1. fertilizer     _____
2. contaminant     _____
3. synthetic     _____
4. additive     _____
5. pellet     _____

   a. 汚染物質
   b. 小球
   c. 合成の
   d. 肥料
   e. 添加物

## 3　VOCABULARY PRACTICE

*Fill in the blanks with the most appropriate word from the box below.*

1. I used _____ to wash my dirty clothes.
2. The architect's plan showed the exact _____ of all the rooms.
3. The fish accidentally ate tiny pieces of _____.
4. The factory's smoke caused _____ in the air.
5. She received a letter from an _____ sender.

> unknown   microplastic   detergent   pollution   dimensions

# ❚❚▶ LISTENING (Input Information)

## 1　NOTE TAKING

[Time 01:29]  21

*Watch the video, listen to the recording, and fill in the blanks with the most appropriate words.*

---

### Microplastic Pollution

1. Microplastics
   - Plastic particles smaller than ₁_____ mm

     e.g., ₂_____, polyethylene

---

2. Sources

- 3_____ products

  e.g., shower gels, 4_____, fertilizers,

  5_____, paint

- 6_____ textiles: release microplastics during

  the 7_____ cycle

- Car tire 8_____

3. Widespread Contamination

- Rivers, 9_____, land, 10_____

4. Persistence and Environmental Impact

- Plastic waste items: take 11_____ of years to break down

- Littering 12_____

- Ingested by species in the ocean

  e.g., zooplankton, 13_____

- Unknown impact on organisms and 14_____

5. Additives in Microplastics

- Contain potential 15_____ contaminants

---

## 2 | COMPREHENSION QUESTIONS

*Write T if the statement is true and F if it is false.*

1. Microplastics are small pieces of plastic, smaller than 5 millimeters in size. _____

2. Nylon and polyethylene are not microplastics; they are made from large pellets. _____

3. Synthetic clothes release very few microplastics when washed. _____

4. Worn car tires contribute to microplastic pollution. _____

5. We don't fully understand how microplastics affect organisms or ecosystems. _____

# **III▶ SPEAKING** (Exchange Ideas)

**1 SPEAKING PRACTICE**     22, 23

*There are diverse opinions about microplastic pollution. Listen to the two dialogs and practice them with your partner. Then think about your views about microplastic pollution. Which opinion is closer to your own?*

## The Impact of Microplastics on Human Health and Preventive Measures

|  | DIALOG 1 | DIALOG 2 |
|---|---|---|
| **Kei** | Have you heard about microplastics? They're harmful. | How can we reduce microplastics? |
| **Emi** | Yes, they're worrying. How do they get in the air? | Use fewer disposable plastics—try reusable bags and bottles. |
| **Kei** | Mainly from washing synthetic clothes and worn-out tires. | What about microbeads in products? |
| **Emi** | What's their impact? | Avoid them. Check labels for polyethylene or polypropylene. |
| **Kei** | Not fully known, but they end up in the food chain, affecting health. | And what about plastic fibers from clothes? |
| **Emi** | We should use less plastic and recycle more. | That's true. Use special bags or filters when washing. |

**2 CREATE A DIALOG**

*Think about how to reduce microplastics based on your own opinions. Complete the following dialog and practice it with your partner.*

## Reducing Microplastics

**You:**          Do you usually try to use less plastic?

**Your partner:** (Yes / No) _____

**You:**          (Why do you / Why don't you) _____

**Your partner:** _____

**You:** (What else do you think…) _____

**Your partner:** _____

# Ⅳ PRESENTATION (Output Your Ideas)

**Argument Points** 〉 Microplastics' Impact on Human Health and Preventive Measures

### Process 1  Research

*Search the Internet or use other means to find which materials release microplastics, their impact on our health, and how we can reduce them. Then think about your own opinions on the subject.*

### Process 2  Brainstorming

*What are your opinions about microplastic pollution? In the following diagram, summarize the information you have researched. Add your own ideas as needed.*

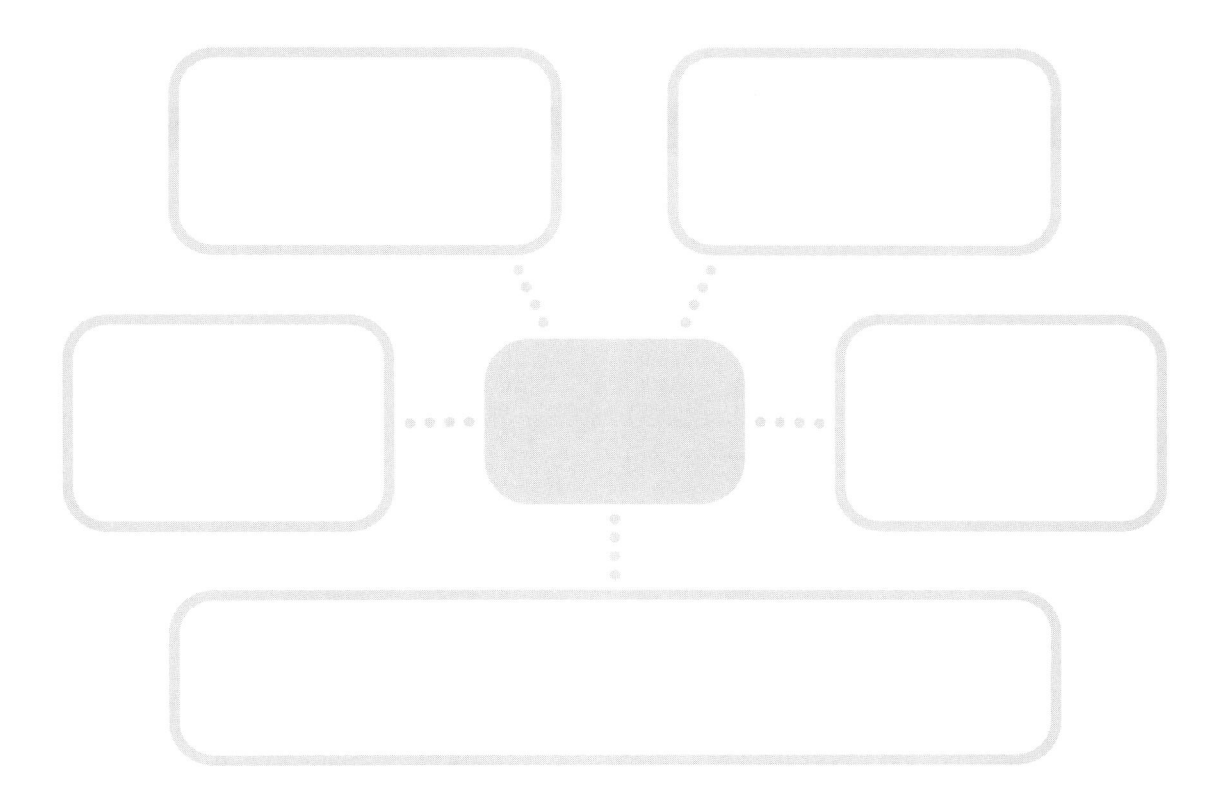

*Summarize what you have researched and the ideas you have come up with in Process 1 and 2 and compose a presentation according to the following outline.*

## Outline

### I. Introduction

**1.** Greeting

_____

**2.** Opening

_____

**3.** Thesis Statement

_____

**4.** Previewing

_____

↓

### II. Body

**1.** Main Idea 1

**2.** Main Idea 2

**3.** Main Idea 3

↓

## III. Conclusion

**1.** Indicating the End

**2.** Summary

**3.** Closing

Process 4  Presenting

*Based on the outline you have created, present it to the entire class.*

# 身振り手振りを活用する

身振り手振りを活用し、視覚的に印象づけます。身振り手振りを活用することで話の魅力や説得力を高めることができます。

## ❶ 手のジェスチャー

手のジェスチャーを使って、ポイントや重要なアイディアを強調します。手を広げたり、指差したり、軽く叩いたりすることで、視覚的なインパクトを与えることができます。

## ❷ 肩や身体の動き

肩や身体の動きを使って、エネルギーや情熱を表現します。大きな身体の動きや軽やかなステップなどを取り入れることで、プレゼンテーションに活気を与えることができます。

## ❸ 表情の変化

表情の変化を使って、感情や意図を伝えます。笑顔や驚き、真剣さなどの表情を使って、聴衆とのつながりを深めることができます。

## ❹ 目の動き

目の動きを使って、聴衆との視覚的な接触を図ります。聴衆の中に目を配り、視線を合わせることで、関心を引き付けることができます。

## ❺ ボディランゲージ

身体のポーズや姿勢を使って、自信や専門性を表現します。立ち姿勢や背筋を伸ばすことで、自信を持ってプレゼンテーションを行うことができます。

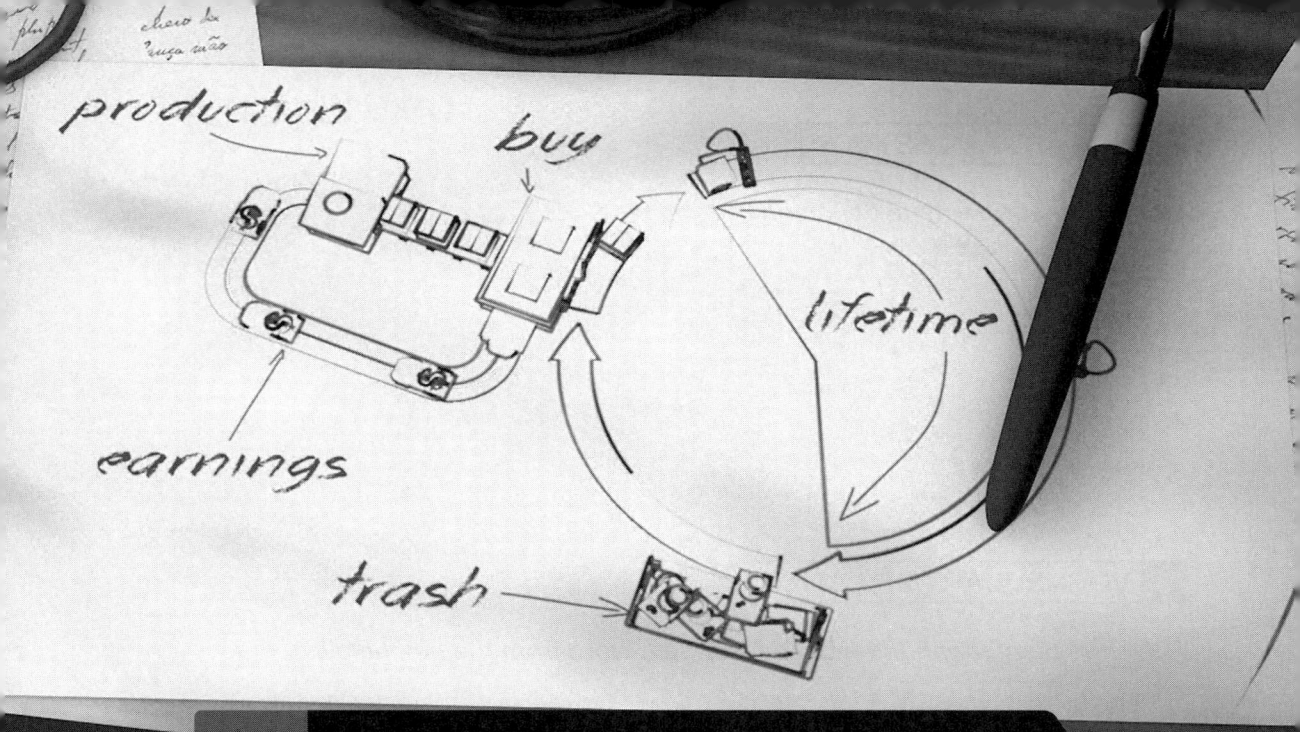

# Planned Obsolescence

Unit
8

Planned Obsolescence（計画的な陳腐化）とは、製品が意図的に寿命を短く設定され、定期的な交換やアップグレードを促す戦略です。消費者に新しい製品を購入させることで市場を活性化させますが、環境への負荷や資源の浪費といった問題も抱えています。計画的な陳腐化の環境や経済活動への影響について考えましょう。

# ▌ WARM-UP

## 1 OPENING QUESTIONS

*Answer the following questions in English.*

1. Have you heard of planned obsolescence?

2. What are the environmental consequences of planned obsolescence?

3. How does planned obsolescence impact consumers financially?

## 2 VOCABULARY STUDY

*Match the word with its definition in Japanese.*

1. depletion  _____
2. compatible  _____
3. emission  _____
4. appliance  _____
5. stimulate  _____

a. 刺激する
b. 枯渇
c. 互換性のある
d. 電化製品
e. 排出

## 3 VOCABULARY PRACTICE

*Fill in the blanks with the most appropriate word from the box below.*

1. The factory was fined for releasing _____ waste into the river.

2. Governments have been trying to make the _____ more eco-friendly than before.

3. The loud music _____ the people, making them want to dance.

4. The _____ of a bridge is how long it is from one side to the other.

5. The magician made the rabbit _____ from the hat.

> stimulated    toxic    landfill    vanish    span

# ▮▶ LISTENING (Input Information)

## 1 NOTE TAKING

[Time 01:58]    24

*Watch the video, listen to the recording, and fill in the blanks with the most appropriate words.*

---

### Understanding Planned Obsolescence

1. Origin and Concept
   - Coined in the United States in 1932
   - During an economic 1 _____

---

- For stimulating 2_____ by limiting the life

  3_____ of consumer goods

2. Implementation by Manufacturers

   - Household 4_____, computers, and electronics

   - Limiting product life spans or make 5_____ impossible

   - Encouragement of 6_____ items

3. Types of Obsolescence

   - Software obsolescence: 7_____ issues with new software

   - Aesthetic obsolescence: 8_____ versions

4. Environmental Impact

   - Screen manufacturing: significant 9_____ impact

   - Depletion of 10_____

   - Damage to 11_____

5. Electronic Waste

   - Electronic and electrical waste in 2016: 12_____ million tons

   - Recycled waste: only 13_____%

6. Legal Actions

   - 14_____ under the law in 15_____ since 2015

## 2  COMPREHENSION QUESTIONS

*Write T if the statement is true and F if it is false.*

1. Planned obsolescence is a new concept.                                                   _____

2. Bernard London suggested forcing products to wear out to slow industrial growth.                                                   _____

3. Planned obsolescence aims to make people buy new things often.                                                   _____

4. Aesthetic obsolescence isn't about software compatibility.                                                   _____

5. In 2016, just 20 percent of electronic waste was recycled globally.                                                   _____

# ▥ SPEAKING (Exchange Ideas)

## 1 SPEAKING PRACTICE

EC CD 25, 26

*There are diverse opinions about planned obsolescence. Listen to the two dialogs and practice them with your partner. Then think about your own views about planned obsolescence. Which opinion is closer to your own?*

## The Pros and Cons of Planned Obsolescence

| | DIALOG 1 | DIALOG 2 |
|---|---|---|
| Kei | Have you heard about planned obsolescence? | What do you think about planned obsolescence? |
| Emi | Yes, it's when products are designed to have a limited lifespan, right? | It's not great because it makes us buy more things and throw away stuff unnecessarily. |
| Kei | Exactly. One advantage is that it stimulates innovation. | Yes, and it means we have to replace our things more often. |
| Emi | That's true. It encourages companies to constantly improve their products. | It also makes more junk that can harm nature and people. |
| Kei | Plus, frequent upgrades can lead to job creation and economic growth. | Right, throwing away old gadgets can be bad for the planet and our health. |
| Emi | That's a good point. It keeps industries competitive and drives technological advancements. | And it's annoying when things break quickly and we always have to buy new ones. |

## 2 CREATE A DIALOG

*Think about the problems of planned obsolescence based on your own opinions. Complete the following dialog and practice it with your partner.*

## Solution for the Problems of Planned Obsolescence

**You:** How can we reduce the impact of planned obsolescence?

**Your partner:** _____

You: _____

Your partner: _____

You: _____

Your partner: _____

# Ⅳ PRESENTATION (Output Your Ideas)

**Argument Points** The Pros and Cons of Planned Obsolescence

**Process 1 Research**

*Search the Internet or use other means to learn about the benefits and problems of planned obsolescence and their impact on our lives. Then think about your own opinions on the subject.*

**Process 2 Brainstorming**

*What are your opinions about planned obsolescence? In the following diagram, summarize the information you have researched. Add your own ideas as needed.*

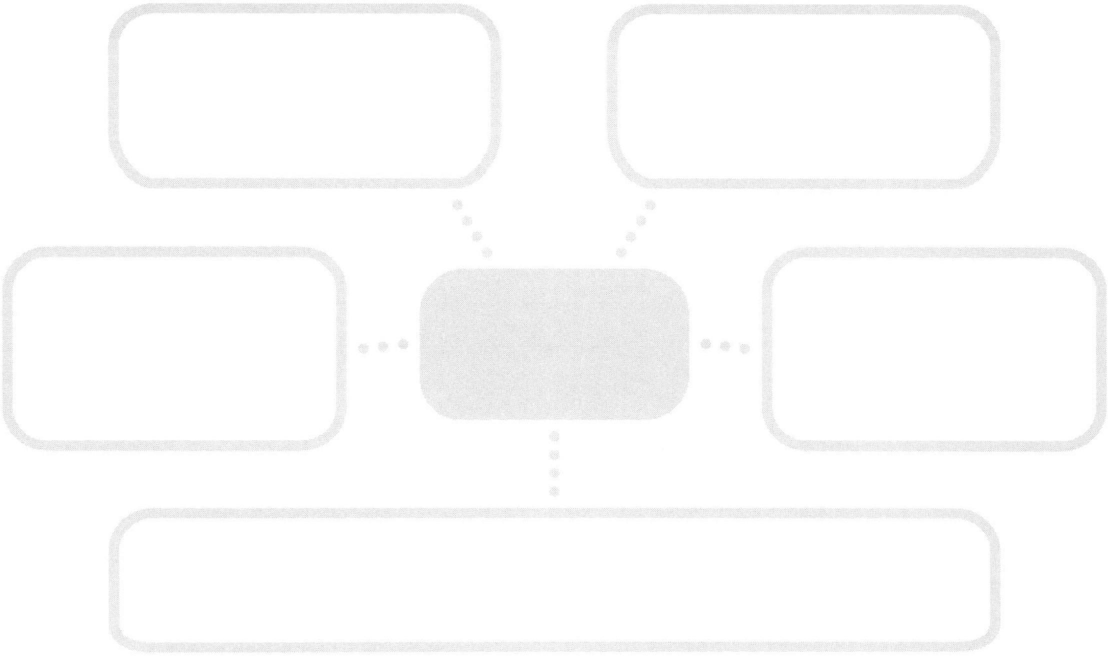

*Summarize what you have researched and the ideas you have come up with in Process 1 and 2 and compose a presentation according to the following outline.*

## Outline

### I. Introduction

**1.** Greeting

_____

**2.** Opening

_____

**3.** Thesis Statement

_____

**4.** Previewing

_____

↓

### II. Body

**1.** Main Idea 1

**2.** Main Idea 2

**3.** Main Idea 3

↓

## III. Conclusion

**1.** Indicating the End

**2.** Summary

**3.** Closing

Process 4   Presenting

*Based on the outline you have created, present it to the entire class.*

# 音量とスピードに気を付ける

適切な音量とスピードで話し、聴衆に理解されやすくします。

### ❶練習を重ねる

練習を重ねて、プレゼンテーションのスピードや音量を調整しましょう。練習を通じて、自分がどのようなペースで話せば聴衆が理解しやすいかを確認することができます。

### ❷スピーカーの設定を確認する

プレゼンテーションを行う場所で、スピーカーの設定を確認してください。適切な音量で聞き取れるように調整することが大切です。

### ❸口の中でゆっくりと話す

口の中でゆっくりと話すことで、スピードをコントロールしましょう。意識的に息を吸い込んだり、言葉の間に適度なポーズを入れたりすることで、聴衆が理解しやすいペースで話すことができます。

### ❹大きな音量で話す必要はない

大きな音量で話す必要はありません。適度な音量で話すことが大切です。強調したい箇所で音量を上げることもできます。

### ❺無理をしない

スピードや音量に無理をしないでください。自然な形で話すことが重要です。無理をすることで、聴衆に不快感を与えたり、プレゼンテーションの内容を理解しにくくすることがあります。

# Autonomous Cars: Hands on the Wheel for Now...

**Unit 9**

自動運転車の発展は、自動車産業に革新的な変化をもたらしています。これらの車両は先進的なセンサーとソフトウェア技術を活用し、運転者の介入なしで自律的に操作できるように進化しています。急激な発展にもかかわらず、現在の段階では運転者は引き続き全面的な責任を持っています。自動運転車の安全性や事故の責任など、発展に伴う問題点も考えましょう。

# ▌▶ WARM-UP

## 1 | OPENING QUESTIONS

*Answer the following questions in English.*

1. What do you know about autonomous cars?

_____

2. Would you like to buy an autonomous car?

_____

3. What are some potential benefits of self-driving technology?

_____

## 2 | VOCABULARY STUDY

*Match the word with its definition in Japanese.*

1. adaptive _____
2. autonomous _____
3. circumstance _____
4. simultaneously _____
5. steer _____

a. 自律的な
b. （ハンドルで）操舵する
c. 適応性のある
d. 同時に
e. 環境、境遇

## 3 | VOCABULARY PRACTICE

*Fill in the blanks with the most appropriate word from the box below.*

1. A thermometer is an _____ of the temperature.
2. The healthcare _____ is growing rapidly.
3. The car's _____ were not working properly, so they needed to be repaired.
4. The car's _____ was impressive, going from 0 to 60 mph in just a few seconds.
5. He learned how to _____ the new machinery at the factory.

> acceleration    indicator    operate    sector    brakes

# II▶ LISTENING (Input Information)

## 1 | NOTE TAKING

[Time 02:03]  27

*Watch the video, listen to the recording, and fill in the blanks with the most appropriate words.*

---

### Six Levels of Driving Automation

Autonomous Vehicles: The Future of Car 1_____

[Level 0]    • Limited 2_____ features

---

e.g., automatic 3_____ braking

[Level 1] • Driver: gets 4_____, brake, or 5_____ support

e.g., lane 6_____ or adaptive cruise control, not simultaneously

[Level 2] • At least two autonomous tasks simultaneously

e.g., 7_____ and acceleration

• Driver: must remain 8_____

[Level 3] • Vehicle: manages most driving functions in limited circumstances

e.g., traffic 9_____

• Driver: must 10_____ when prompted

[Level 4] • Vehicle: no steering 11_____

• Fully automated, operates in most road 12_____

e.g., driverless taxi or 13_____

[Level 5] • Vehicle: drives itself in all environments, day or night, and any

14_____ conditions

• Fully 15_____ vehicle, no driver intervention required

## 2  COMPREHENSION QUESTIONS

*Write T if the statement is true and F if it is false.*

1. Autonomous vehicles are seen as the future of car transportation.  _____

2. In Level 1 automation, a driver can use lane centering and adaptive cruise control at the same time.  _____

3. Level 3 means the car can handle most driving tasks, and the driver only needs to take over in certain situations like traffic jams.  _____

4. Level 4 means the car has a steering wheel for the passenger to use if needed.  _____

5. Level 5 is a fully automated car that can drive itself anywhere, anytime, and in any weather.  _____

# ▮▮▮ SPEAKING (Exchange Ideas)

## 1 SPEAKING PRACTICE

 28, 29

*There are diverse opinions about self-driving cars. Listen to the two dialogs and practice them with your partner. Then think about your opinions about autonomous driving. Which opinion is closer to your own?*

## The Pros and Cons of Autonomous Driving

| | DIALOG 1 | DIALOG 2 |
|---|---|---|
| **Kei** | Have you heard about self-driving cars? | What do you think about self-driving cars? |
| **Emi** | Yes, they seem useful. | Not sure. They sound a bit scary. |
| **Kei** | They might reduce accidents by following rules. | What if they make mistakes? |
| **Emi** | That's great. It helps those who can't drive. | Or if hackers take control? |
| **Kei** | But what if they fail? That's risky. | It could also take jobs from taxi drivers. |
| **Emi** | True, but engineers are focused on safety. | True, there's a lot to consider. |

## 2 CREATE A DIALOG

*Think about the use of self-driving technology based on your opinions. Complete the following dialog and practice it with your partner.*

## Self-driving Technology

**You:** Have you ever heard about that accident involving an autonomous car before?

**Your partner:** (Yes / No) _____?

**You:** I think it's a tricky situation. _____

**Your partner:** (human oversight…) _____

**You:**       (the human driver should take control if needed) _____

**Your partner:** _____

# Ⅳ▶ PRESENTATION (Output Your Ideas)

**Argument Points** ⟩ **Autonomous Driving: Advantages, Disadvantages, and Responsibility**

**Process 1    Research**

*Search the Internet or use other means to find what levels of autonomous driving are available now, what impact they have on our society, how we can rely on the technology. Then think about your own opinions on the subject.*

**Process 2    Brainstorming**

*What are your opinions about autonomous cars? In the following diagram, summarize the information you have researched. Add your own ideas as needed.*

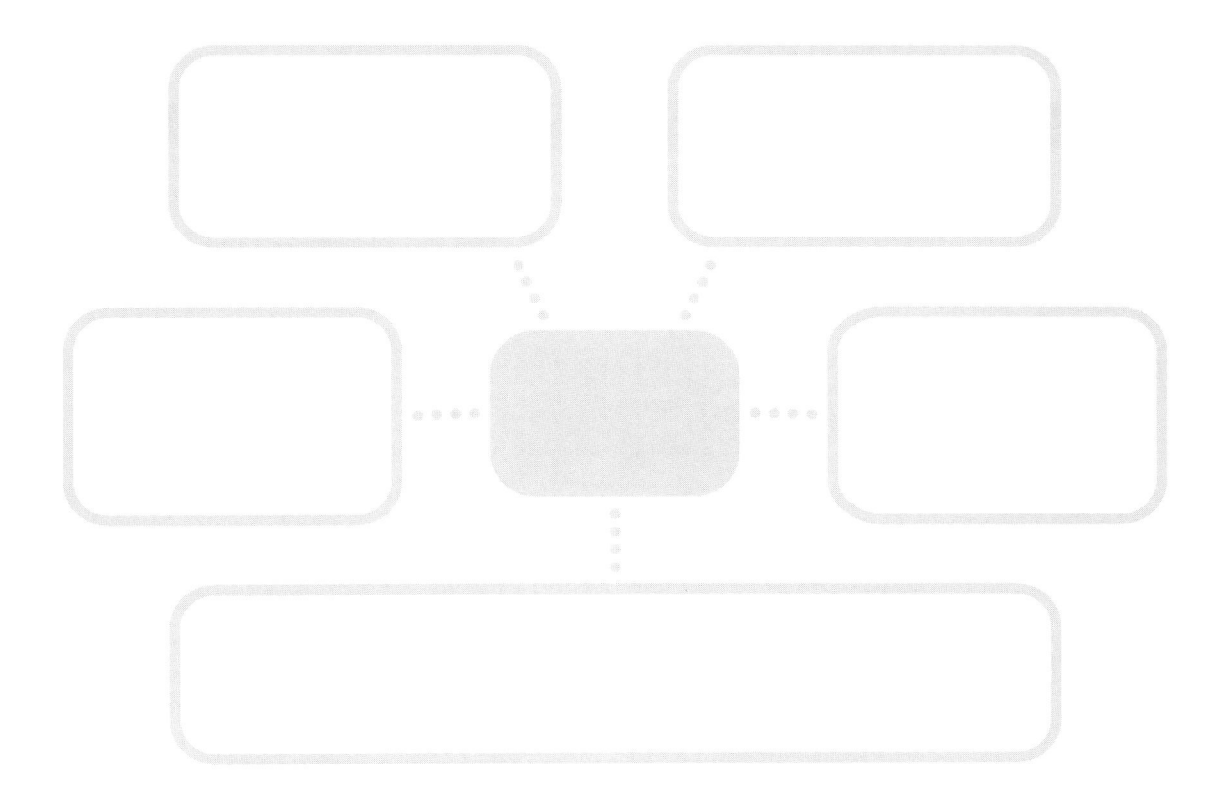

*Summarize what you have researched and the ideas you have come up with in Process 1 and 2 and compose a presentation according to the following outline.*

## Outline

### I. Introduction

**1.** Greeting

_____

**2.** Opening

_____

**3.** Thesis Statement

_____

**4.** Previewing

_____

↓

### II. Body

**1.** Main Idea 1

|  |
|--|
|  |

**2.** Main Idea 2

|  |
|--|
|  |

**3.** Main Idea 3

<br>
<br>

$\downarrow$

### III. Conclusion

**1.** Indicating the End

**2.** Summary

**3.** Closing

**Process 4** **Presenting**

*Based on the outline you have created, present it to the entire class.*

# 資料を活用する

> グラフや図表など、視覚的な資料を活用することで、視聴者に印象づけます。

## ❶ スライドプレゼンテーション

スライドを使って主要なポイントや情報を視覚的に提示します。テキスト、画像、グラフ、チャートなどを使って、聴衆が理解しやすい形で情報を伝えることができます。

## ❷ ビデオやオーディオクリップの挿入

ビデオやオーディオクリップを使用して、特定の概念や事例を具体的に説明することができます。関連する動画や音声素材を活用し、聴衆の興味を引きつけることができます。

## ❸ グラフやチャートの表示

データや統計を視覚的に表現するために、グラフやチャートを使用します。適切なグラフやチャートを選んでデータを表示することで、情報をわかりやすく整理し、聴衆に効果的に伝えることができます。

## ❹ プロップの使用

プロップ（小道具）を使って、具体的な物を示すことができます。例えば、モデル、図表、実際の製品などを使って、説明やデモンストレーションを行うことができます。

## ❺ ハンドアウトや参考資料の提供

プレゼンテーション後に聴衆にハンドアウトや参考資料を提供することで、詳細な情報を提供することができます。資料には追加の情報や参考文献、重要なポイントのまとめなどが含まれます。

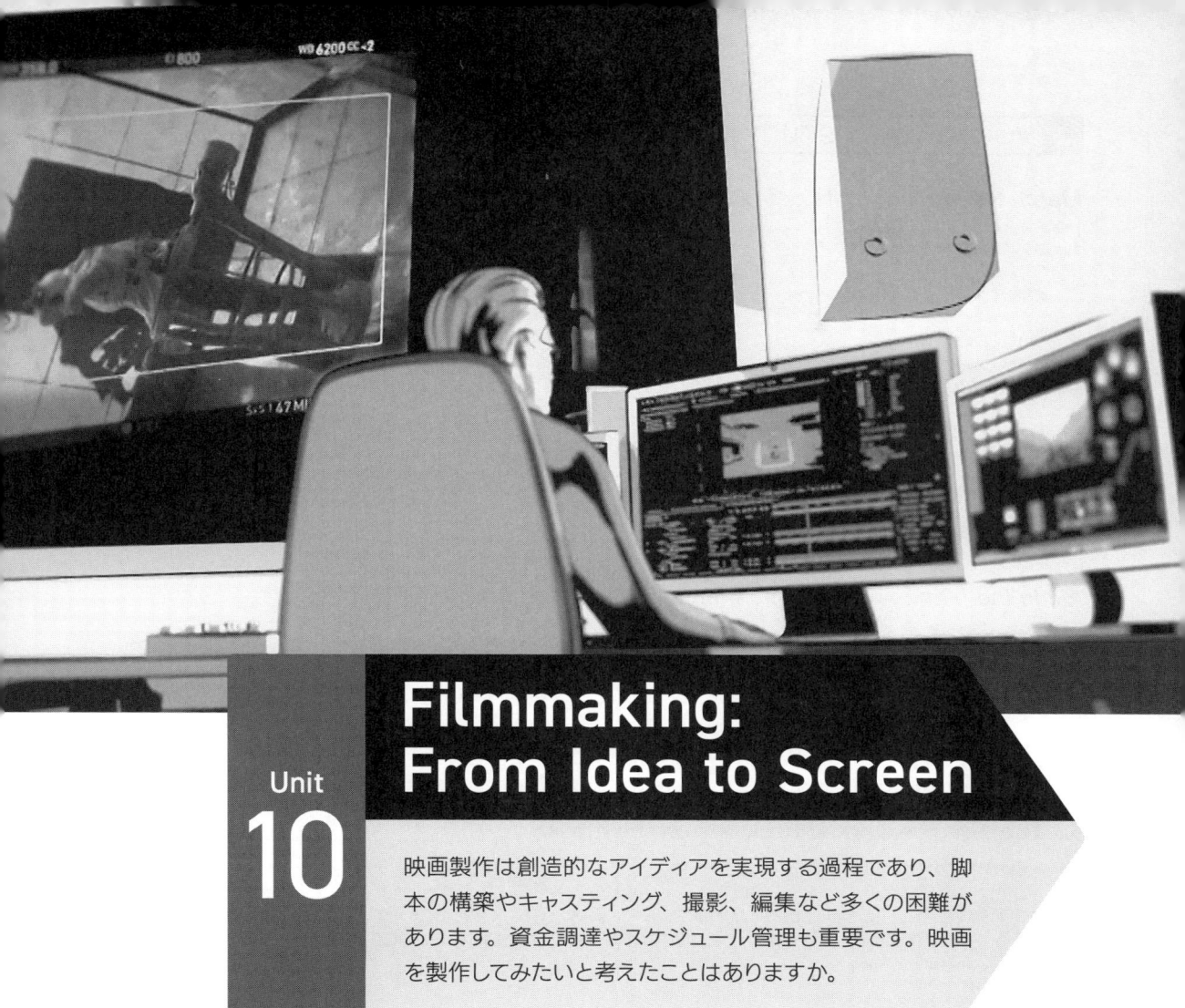

## Unit 10

### Filmmaking: From Idea to Screen

映画製作は創造的なアイディアを実現する過程であり、脚本の構築やキャスティング、撮影、編集など多くの困難があります。資金調達やスケジュール管理も重要です。映画を製作してみたいと考えたことはありますか。

## ▶ WARM-UP

### 1 OPENING QUESTIONS

*Answer the following questions in English.*

1. What are some key steps involved in the process of filmmaking?

2. Why is scriptwriting considered an essential part of filmmaking?

3. How does effective casting contribute to the success of a film?

## 2 │ VOCABULARY STUDY

*Match the word with its definition in Japanese.*

1. accommodation _____
2. cater _____
3. patience _____
4. spectacular _____
5. finance _____

a. 料理を調達する
b. 壮観
c. 宿泊施設
d. 資金を調達する
e. 忍耐

## 3 │ VOCABULARY PRACTICE

*Fill in the blanks with the most appropriate word from the box below.*

1. The sports commentator provided live _____ during the game.
2. She took a perfect _____ of the sunset with her camera.
3. A good handbag is both a stylish _____ and a practical item.
4. The astronauts' _____ to Mars lasted several months.
5. The director worked tirelessly on the film's _____ to ensure a compelling story.

> screenplay   snap   commentary   mission   accessory

# ▐▌▶ LISTENING (Input Information)

## 1 │ NOTE TAKING

[Time 02:13] WEB動画 EC DVD CD 30

*Watch the video, listen to the recording, and fill in the blanks with the most appropriate words.*

### Filmmaking Process

1. Starting Point

   - 1_____ idea
   - Filmmaker, 2_____, producer, scriptwriter, author
   - Choosing the 3_____

2. Screenplay Development

- Producer's involvement
- Mission: driving filmmaking within 4_____

3. Funding and Distribution

- Securing funding from 5_____, public finances, sponsors
- Identifying distributors

4. Pre-production Logistics

- First assistant director: creates and manages 6_____ schedule
- Location 7_____

5. Crew and Casting

- Executive producer: assembling film crew
- Casting director: hires 8_____ and 9_____

6. Filming

- Director, 10_____ team, sound crew
- Set 11_____, on-site logistics team

7. Post-Production

- Rushes selection: frames chosen for 12_____
- Sound mix: sound effects, 13_____, music
- Special effects   • Calibration in the 14_____ room

8. Final Approval and Release

- Director, producer, distributors: agree on the final 15_____
- Film completion

---

## 2 | COMPREHENSION QUESTIONS

*Write T if the statement is true and F if it is false.*

1. Making a film requires talent, team spirit, and patience.                    _____

2. The screenplay is developed before the plot is chosen.                    _____

3. It is the producer's job to make the filming schedule.                    _____

4. The first assistant director is in charge of managing the film crew.                    _____

5. Post-production means adding sound effects and music to make
   the film feel more alive.                    _____

# ▐▐▌ SPEAKING (Exchange Ideas)

## 1 SPEAKING PRACTICE

EC CD 31, 32

*There are diverse opinions about filmmaking. Listen to the two dialogs and practice them with your partner. Then think about your opinions about filmmaking. Which opinion is closer to your own?*

## Fun and Challenges of Filmmaking

| | DIALOG 1 | DIALOG 2 |
|---|---|---|
| **Kei** | Filmmaking seems like a lot of fun. | Filmmaking has its challenges. |
| **Emi** | Yes, it is. Thinking of creative ideas and making them real is exciting. | Yes, it's not as easy as people think. There are many problems. |
| **Kei** | Working with a team to make it happen must be enjoyable. | Like getting money and managing the budget? |
| **Emi** | It sure is. Working with talented people is great. | Exactly. Budgeting money can be hard, and organizing schedules and logistics takes a lot of work. |
| **Kei** | And seeing the final movie on the big screen is very satisfying. | It does. Making sure everything goes well is tough. |
| **Emi** | It's like seeing your dreams come true. | But despite the problems, the end result is usually worth it. |

## 2 CREATE A DIALOG

*Think about the dreams of filmmaking based on your own opinions. Complete the following dialog and practice it with your partner.*

## Dreams of Filmmaking

**You:** Have you ever dreamed of becoming a filmmaker?

**Your partner:** (Yes / No) _____

**You:** _____

Your partner: _____

You: _____

Your partner: _____

# **IV** PRESENTATION (Output Your Ideas)

**Argument Points** The Enjoyment and Challenges of Filmmaking

### Process 1 Research

*Search the Internet or use other means to discover what fun and challenges filmmaking has, and its impact on our lives. Then think about your own opinions on the subject.*

### Process 2 Brainstorming

*What are your opinions about filmmaking? In the following diagram, summarize the information you have researched. Add your own ideas as needed.*

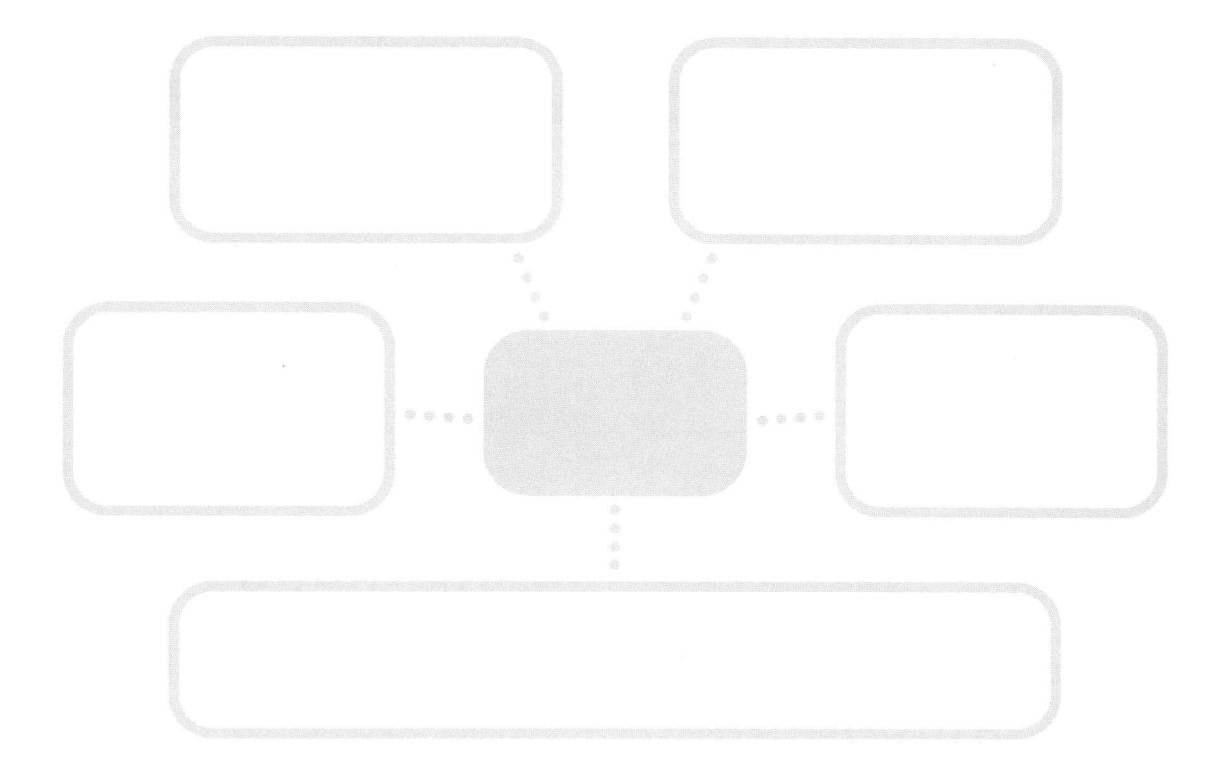

*Summarize what you have researched and the ideas you have come up with in Process 1 and 2 and compose a presentation according to the following outline.*

## Outline

### I. Introduction

1. Greeting

   _____

2. Opening

   _____

3. Thesis Statement

   _____

4. Previewing

   _____

↓

### II. Body

1. Main Idea 1

   [                                               ]

2. Main Idea 2

   [                                               ]

**3.** Main Idea 3

↓

## III. Conclusion

**1.** Indicating the End

**2.** Summary

**3.** Closing

Process 4   Presenting

*Based on the outline you have created, present it to the entire class.*

# 自信を持って話す

> 自信を持って話し、視聴者に信頼感を与えます。

### ❶プレゼンの準備を行う

自信を持って話すためには、プレゼンテーションの準備をしっかり行うことが大切です。しっかりとした資料作りや練習によって、自信を持って話せるようになります。

### ❷目を見て話す

プレゼンテーションを行う際には、聴衆と目を合わせて話すようにしましょう。目を見て話すことで、聴衆とのつながりを感じられるため、自信を持って話せます。

### ❸トーンを上げる

話し方が単調だと、聴衆が飽きてしまいます。トーンを上げることで、聴衆を引きつけることができます。自然なトーンで話すことが大切です。

### ❹ポーズ (間) をとる

プレゼンテーション中にポーズ (間) をとることで、話を整理し、聴衆の注意を引くことができます。ポーズをとることで、自信を持って話せるようになります。

### ❺緊張をコントロールする

プレゼンテーションを行う際には、緊張することがあります。緊張をコントロールするためには、深呼吸をする、リラックスするためのテクニックを身につけることが大切です。緊張をコントロールできると、自信を持って話せるようになります。

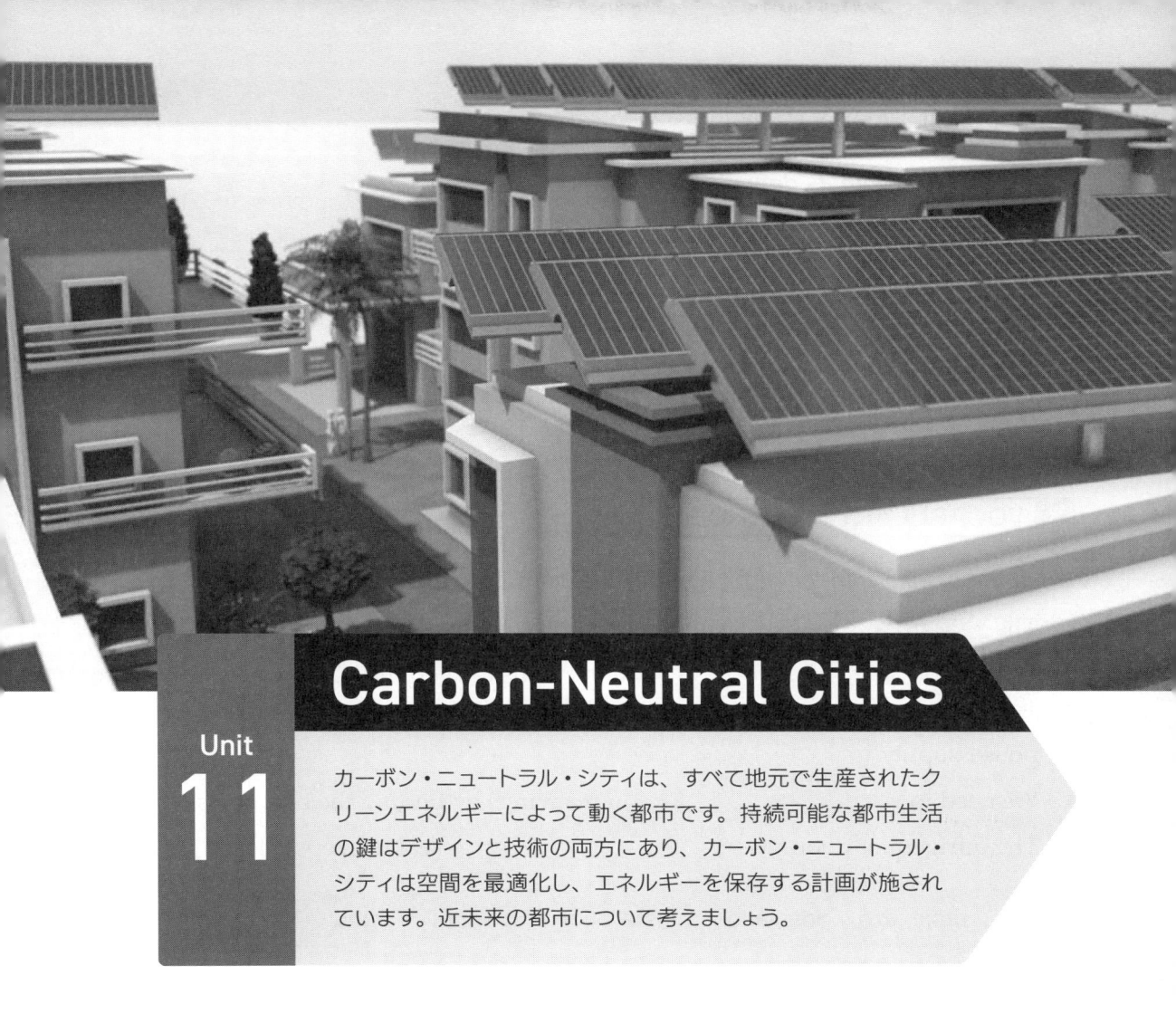

# Carbon-Neutral Cities

カーボン・ニュートラル・シティは、すべて地元で生産されたクリーンエネルギーによって動く都市です。持続可能な都市生活の鍵はデザインと技術の両方にあり、カーボン・ニュートラル・シティは空間を最適化し、エネルギーを保存する計画が施されています。近未来の都市について考えましょう。

# ⓘ WARM-UP

## 1 OPENING QUESTIONS

*Answer the following questions in English.*

1. What do you know about carbon-neutral cities?

   _____

2. What are the key features contributing to a carbon-neutral city's success in promoting green living?

   _____

3. Would you like to live in a carbon-neutral city? Why or why not?

   _____

## 2 VOCABULARY STUDY

*Match the word with its definition in Japanese.*

1. sewage _____
2. ferry _____
3. irrigation _____
4. corridor _____
5. norm _____

a. 現地まで輸送する
b. 一般的水準、主流
c. 廊下、通路
d. 灌漑
e. 汚水

## 3 VOCABULARY PRACTICE

*Fill in the blanks with the most appropriate word from the box below.*

1. The _____ of the new software took only a few minutes.

2. We added _____ to the walls to keep the house warmer in winter.

3. The city plans to upgrade the electrical _____ to improve the power supply.

4. We need to _____ our savings by finding the best deals.

5. The refrigerator door has a _____ seal to keep it closed.

maximize   insulation   installation   magnetic   grid

# II▶ LISTENING (Input Information)

## 1 NOTE TAKING

[Time 01:41]  33

*Watch the video, listen to the recording, and fill in the blanks with the most appropriate words.*

---

### Carbon-Neutral Cities: Sustainable Urban Living

1. Clean Energy
   - Locally produced
   - Wind parks, solar panels

---

- Biogas plants 1_____ by cattle manure and vegetable waste

2. Transport System
   - Driverless
   - Pod cars guided by 2_____ sensors   • Underground corridors

3. Energy-Efficient Homes
   - 3_____ sensors   • Reducing electricity and water 4_____

4. Waste Management
   - Use of treated 5_____ effluent for landscaping
   - Use of 6_____ at waste-to-energy plants

5. Sustainable Urban Design
   - Optimization of 7_____ and conservation of 8_____
   - Use of 9_____ cement for buildings
   - Photovoltaic 10_____

6. Ecological Landscaping
   - Minimal 11_____   • Priority on the 12_____ water cycle

7. Community Engagement
   - For keeping the city 13_____
   - Community building   • Healthy 14_____

## 2  COMPREHENSION QUESTIONS

*Write T if the statement is true and F if it is false.*

1. In a carbon-neutral city, the transportation system uses
   regular vehicles with drivers.                                    _____

2. Home sensors don't control building temperatures.                 _____

3. Sustainable city living relies on both design and technology.     _____

4. Buildings use eco-friendly cement to help the environment.        _____

5. The city's landscaping is planned to water plants efficiently.    _____

# **III ▶ SPEAKING** (Exchange Ideas)

## **1 SPEAKING PRACTICE**

 34, 35

*There are diverse opinions about cities being carbon neutral. Listen to the two dialogs and practice them with your partner. Then think about your views about carbon-neutral cities. Which opinion is closer to your own?*

## The Pros and Cons of Carbon-Neutral Cities

|       | DIALOG 1 |       | DIALOG 2 |
|-------|----------|-------|----------|
| Kei   | Have you heard of carbon-neutral cities? |       | What do you think about carbon-neutral cities? |
| Emi   | Yes, they're cities that aim to have zero carbon emissions. |       | They have benefits, but they can be costly to set up. |
| Kei   | Right. They're great for fighting climate change. |       | Yeah, switching to clean energy and upgrading infrastructure needs a lot of money. |
| Emi   | That's good. I heard they use clean energy too. |       | Some say the technology for carbon neutrality isn't ready yet. |
| Kei   | Yes, like solar and wind power. |       | That's a concern. It might take time to get it right. |
| Emi   | That's great for the environment and reduces our use of fossil fuels. |       | Plus, not everyone may want to use eco-friendly practices. |

## **2 CREATE A DIALOG**

*Think about problems with carbon-neutral cities based on your own views. Complete the following dialog and practice it with your partner.*

## **Problems with Carbon-Neutral Cities**

**You:**　　　What do you think might be the problems with carbon-neutral cities?

**Your partner:** One problem is _____

**You:**　　　Yes, and _____

Your partner: _____

You: _____

Your partner: _____

# **IV** PRESENTATION (Output Your Ideas)

**Argument Points** **The Pros and Cons of Carbon-Neutral Cities**

**Process 1   Research**

*Search the Internet or use other means to find the advantages and disadvantages of carbon-neutral cities. Then think about your own opinions on the subject.*

**Process 2   Brainstorming**

*What are some of the advantages and disadvantages of carbon-neutral cities? In the following diagram, summarize the information you have researched. Add your own ideas as needed.*

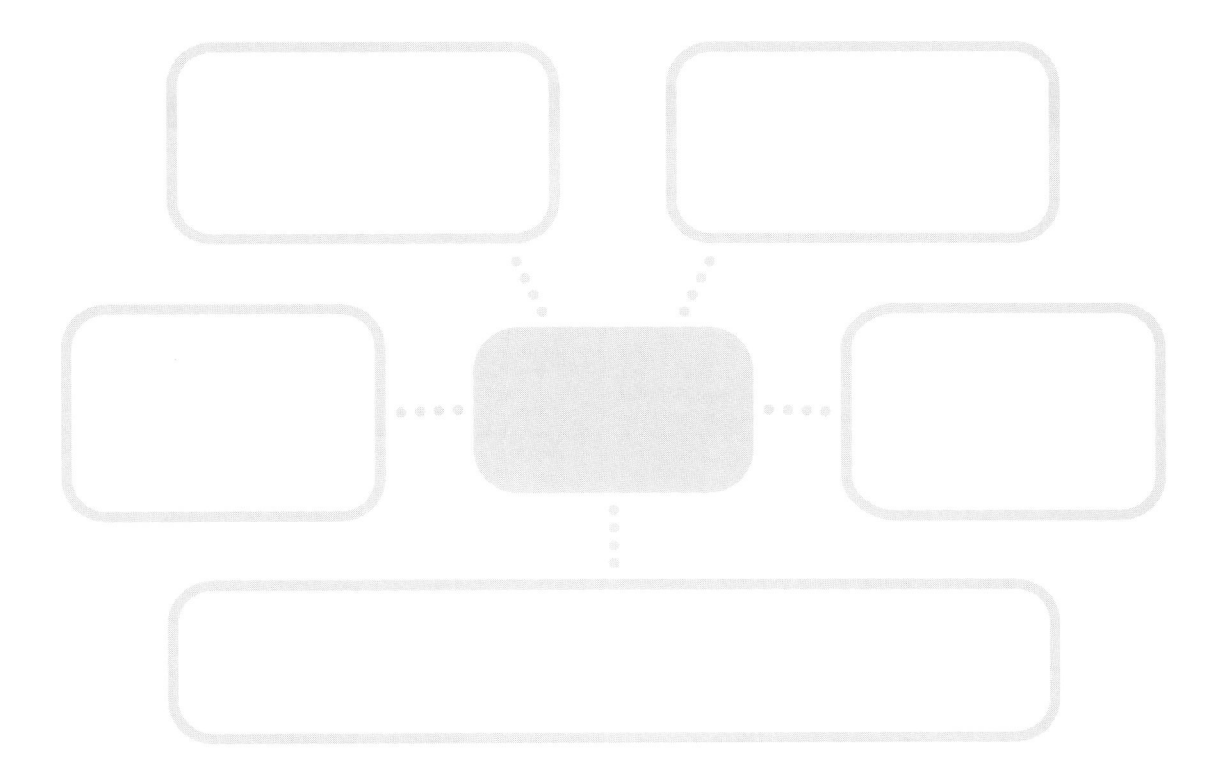

*Summarize what you have researched and the ideas you have come up with in Process 1 and 2 and compose a presentation according to the following outline.*

## Outline

### I. Introduction

**1.** Greeting

_____

**2.** Opening

_____

**3.** Thesis Statement

_____

**4.** Previewing

_____

↓

### II. Body

**1.** Main Idea 1

**2.** Main Idea 2

**3.** Main Idea 3

↓

### III. Conclusion

**1.** Indicating the End

**2.** Summary

**3.** Closing

Process 4　Presenting

*Based on the outline you have created, present it to the entire class.*

# 練習を重ねる

プレゼンテーションをする前に、練習を重ね、自分自身を確信します。

## ❶ 聞き手を立てる

友人や家族など、聞き手を立てて練習することができます。聞き手になる人には、自分自身がプレゼンテーションを聞いたつもりで、フィードバックをしてもらいましょう。

## ❷ タイマーを使う

プレゼンテーションの時間を厳守するために、タイマーを使って練習することが大切です。練習する際には、実際のプレゼンテーションと同じ時間設定をして練習しましょう。

## ❸ 録画してチェックする

スマートフォンなどの録画機能を使って、自分自身のプレゼンテーションを録画し、チェックすることができます。自分自身の話し方や身振り手振りを確認することができます。

## ❹ 読み上げる

プレゼンテーションを読み上げることで、自分自身が書いた文章をより理解し、語彙力を増やすことができます。読み上げることで、プレゼンテーションの流れを確認することができます。

## ❺ フィードバックをもらう

練習したプレゼンテーションを、友人や教師に見てもらい、フィードバックをもらうことができます。フィードバックをもらうことで、改善点を把握し、より良いプレゼンテーションになるように練習することができます。

# The United Nations

国際連合（United Nations）は、世界平和と安全、人権、開発、人道支援などを促進する国際機関です。しかし、国際紛争や紛争地域での課題、開発の不均衡、気候変動、人道危機への対応など、さまざまな課題に直面しています。また、加盟国の意見の一致や実効性の確保など、組織内の課題もあります。

# ▶ WARM-UP

## 1 OPENING QUESTIONS

*Answer the following questions in English.*

1. What is the United Nations?

   _____

2. Where is the headquarters of the United Nations located?

   _____

3. Name one main body of the United Nations and its function.

   _____

## 2 VOCABULARY STUDY

*Match the word with its definition in Japanese.*

1. veto _____
2. pledge _____
3. charter _____
4. declaration _____
5. recommendation _____

a. 宣言
b. 憲章
c. 拒否権
d. 推薦
e. 誓約

## 3 VOCABULARY PRACTICE

*Fill in the blanks with the most appropriate word from the box below.*

1. The business contract is _____ after it ends.
2. After years of negotiations, the conflict finally _____.
3. The UN has different main _____ responsible for various functions.
4. The headquarters of the UN in New York is considered international _____.
5. The court's decision was based on principles of fairness and _____.

> organs    ceased    justice    territory    renewable

# ▌▌▶ LISTENING (Input Information)

## 1 NOTE TAKING

[Time 01:48]     36

*Watch the video, listen to the recording, and fill in the blanks with the most appropriate words.*

### The United Nations

1. Background
   • International organization: promoting world 1_____

- Forerunner: 2_____ of Nations
- The name "United Nations" first used in 3_____

2. **Establishment**

- Charter signed on June 26, 1945 by 4_____ original member states
- Established on 5_____ 24, 1945 upon ratification
- Headquarters in New York: international 6_____

3. **Main Bodies**

- General 7_____
  - Represents all 8_____ member states
  - Key decisions: a 9_____ majority
- Security Council
  - Maintains international peace and 10_____
  - 15 members: 5 11_____, 10 non-permanent
- Economic and Social Council
  - Handles economic, social, and 12_____ issues
- International 13_____ of Justice
  - Principal 14_____ organ
- Secretariat
  - Home to the Secretary-General
  - Appointed for a 15_____ renewable term

---

## 2 COMPREHENSION QUESTIONS

*Write T if the statement is true and F if it is false.*

1. The League of Nations was established after World War II. _____
2. The name "United Nations" was first used during World War II. _____
3. The United Nations Charter was signed on June 26, 1945. _____
4. The Security Council of the United Nations has 20 members. _____
5. The Secretary-General heads the Secretariat of the United Nations. _____

# ▐▶ SPEAKING (Exchange Ideas)

## 1 SPEAKING PRACTICE

  37, 38

*There are diverse opinions about the United Nations. Listen to the two dialogs and practice them with your partner. Then think about your own views about the United Nations. Which opinion is closer to yours?*

## The Pros and Cons of the United Nations

| | DIALOG 1 | DIALOG 2 |
|---|---|---|
| Kei | What do you think are some advantages of the United Nations? | What are some criticisms of the United Nations? |
| Emi | Well, it tries to solve problems without fighting. | With so many different groups, it's hard to get things done quickly. |
| Kei | That's right. The UN helps when conflicts happen in countries. | I agree. Big countries can control decisions, leaving others out. |
| Emi | It also makes sure people are treated fairly everywhere. | And even when they agree on things, making it happen is tough. |
| Kei | The UN cares about making the world healthier and smarter. | People also worry that some UN plans don't work well or aren't fair. |
| Emi | It's important for making the world better for everyone. | So, it's not perfect and needs improvements. |

## 2 CREATE A DIALOG

*Think about the issues the United Nations Security Council should handle based on your own views. Complete the following dialog and practice it with your partner.*

## Issues the United Nations Security Council Should Handle

**You:**　　　　Do you know what issues the United Nations Security Council deals with?

**Your partner:** _____

**You:** _____

Your partner: _____

You: _____

Your partner: _____

# **IV** PRESENTATION (Output Your Ideas)

**Argument Points** ⟩ **Issues the United Nations Should Handle**

**Process 1  Research**

*Search the Internet or use other means to find the benefits and problems of the United Nations and its impact on our lives. Then think about your own opinions on the subject.*

**Process 2  Brainstorming**

*What are your opinions about the United Nations? In the following diagram, summarize the information you have researched. Add your own ideas as needed.*

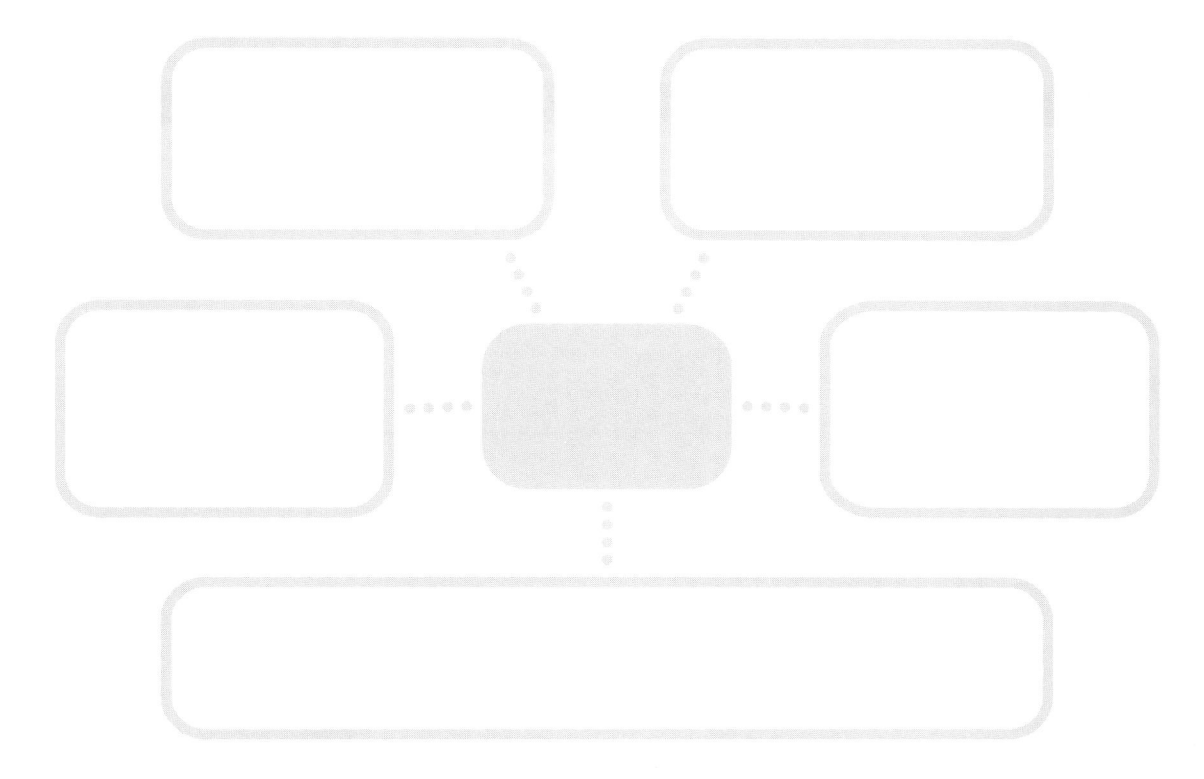

*Summarize what you have researched and the ideas you have come up with in Process 1 and 2 and compose a presentation according to the following outline.*

## Outline

### I. Introduction

**1.** Greeting

---

**2.** Opening

---

**3.** Thesis Statement

---

**4.** Previewing

---

↓

### II. Body

**1.** Main Idea 1

**2.** Main Idea 2

**3.** Main Idea 3

↓

## III. Conclusion

**1.** Indicating the End

**2.** Summary

**3.** Closing

Process 4   Presenting

*Based on the outline you have created, present it to the entire class.*

# 視線を使い分ける

視線を使い分け、聴衆全体を見ながら話すようにします。

### ❶全員に向けた話をする場合
視線をスムーズに移動させ、周囲全体をカバーするようにする。

### ❷特定の人やグループに向けて話す場合
その人やグループに向けてしばらく視線を合わせる。

### ❸資料を見せる場合
視線を資料に向け、必要な情報を見つけやすくする。

### ❹重要なポイントを強調する場合
視線を聴衆全体に向け、そのポイントを印象づける。

### ❺質問に答える場合
質問をした人に向けて視線を合わせ、その後は聴衆全体に向けて話を続ける。

# Appendix

# Presentation Evaluation Rubric

Student Number: _____     Name: _____

Chapter : _____     Topic: _____

| Scoring: 1 – Poor / 2 – Needs Improvement / 3 – Fair / 4 – Good / 5 – Excellent | | |
|---|---|---|
| Preparation | The student met all deadlines and put effort into planning and preparation. | |
| Content | The content of the presentation is interesting and meaningful. | |
| Introduction | The introduction is appropriate and catches the audience's attention. The presenter greets the audience, states the main idea and uses a question, story, fact, or quotation. | |
| Body | The main points or opinions of the body are clear and supported with details and reasons. | |
| Conclusion | The conclusion is appropriate and satisfying for the audience. The presenter gives a final thought on the topic, states the main idea again, and thanks the audience. | |
| Vocabulary | The presenter uses a wide range of vocabulary and phrases. | |
| Speaking Volume | The presenter speaks in a loud and clear voice. | |
| Pronunciation & Intonation | The presenter speaks with emphasis and has good intonation and pronunciation. | |
| Physical message | The presenter makes excellent eye contact, uses a variety of appropriate facial and hand gestures, and maintains good posture. | |
| "Read, Look Up, Present" | The presenter either speaks without a script/notes or uses the "Read, Look Up, Present" technique well. | |
| | Time limit observed: Yes / No     If "No," minus 5 points. | |
| | Total Score | |

**Final Score** _____ /50

Comments: _____

_____

_____

Presentation Evaluation Sheet 1: **General Overview**

| Criteria:  Excellent (5)  Good (4)  Fair (3) Needs Improvement (2)  Poor (1) | | | | | | Comments |
|---|---|---|---|---|---|---|
| Clarity of Purpose | 1 | 2 | 3 | 4 | 5 | |
| Content Quality | 1 | 2 | 3 | 4 | 5 | |
| Organization | 1 | 2 | 3 | 4 | 5 | |
| Visual Aids | 1 | 2 | 3 | 4 | 5 | |
| Audience Engagement | 1 | 2 | 3 | 4 | 5 | |
| Delivery (Voice, Pace) | 1 | 2 | 3 | 4 | 5 | |
| Time Management | 1 | 2 | 3 | 4 | 5 | |
| Overall Impact | 1 | 2 | 3 | 4 | 5 | |

Presentation Evaluation Sheet 2: **Content and Structure**

| Criteria:  Excellent (5)  Good (4)  Fair (3) Needs Improvement (2)  Poor (1) | | | | | | Comments |
|---|---|---|---|---|---|---|
| Introduction | 1 | 2 | 3 | 4 | 5 | |
| Thesis Statement/ Objective | 1 | 2 | 3 | 4 | 5 | |
| Clearly Stated Main Points | 1 | 2 | 3 | 4 | 5 | |
| Logical Flow of Ideas | 1 | 2 | 3 | 4 | 5 | |
| Supporting Evidence/ Examples | 1 | 2 | 3 | 4 | 5 | |
| Conclusion/Summary | 1 | 2 | 3 | 4 | 5 | |

Presentation Evaluation Sheet 3: **Delivery and Engagement**

| Criteria: Excellent (5) Good (4) Fair (3) Needs Improvement (2) Poor (1) | | | | | | Comments |
|---|---|---|---|---|---|---|
| Eye Contact | 1 | 2 | 3 | 4 | 5 | |
| Body Language | 1 | 2 | 3 | 4 | 5 | |
| Voice Projection | 1 | 2 | 3 | 4 | 5 | |
| Pace and Timing | 1 | 2 | 3 | 4 | 5 | |
| Confidence | 1 | 2 | 3 | 4 | 5 | |
| Audience Interaction | 1 | 2 | 3 | 4 | 5 | |

Presentation Evaluation Sheet 4: **Visuals and Technology**

| Criteria: Excellent (5) Good (4) Fair (3) Needs Improvement (2) Poor (1) | | | | | | Comments |
|---|---|---|---|---|---|---|
| Quality of Visual Aids | 1 | 2 | 3 | 4 | 5 | |
| Relevance of Visual Aids | 1 | 2 | 3 | 4 | 5 | |
| Use of Technology | 1 | 2 | 3 | 4 | 5 | |
| Visual Aid Readability | 1 | 2 | 3 | 4 | 5 | |
| Integration with Speech | 1 | 2 | 3 | 4 | 5 | |

Presentation Evaluation Sheet 5: **Overall Effectiveness**

| Criteria:  Excellent (5)  Good (4)  Fair (3)<br>Needs Improvement (2)  Poor (1) | | | | | | Comments |
|---|---|---|---|---|---|---|
| Achieved Purpose | 1 | 2 | 3 | 4 | 5 | |
| Audience Engagement | 1 | 2 | 3 | 4 | 5 | |
| Memorability | 1 | 2 | 3 | 4 | 5 | |
| Persuasiveness | 1 | 2 | 3 | 4 | 5 | |
| Handling of Questions | 1 | 2 | 3 | 4 | 5 | |
| Professionalism | 1 | 2 | 3 | 4 | 5 | |

# プレゼンテーションの論理展開例

## 1 Chronological (Time) Order ［時系列順］

時系列順の論理展開とは、出来事や考え方が起こった順に、古いものから新しいものへと紹介する方法です。このアプローチは、物語や歴史的な出来事の説明に特に効果的です。聴衆が時間の流れに沿って情報を理解しやすくなるため、出来事の進展や因果関係が明確になります。

| 基本構造 | |
| --- | --- |
| 導入<br>(Introduction) | 説明する出来事や考え方の全体像を簡潔に紹介します。 |
| 時系列の出来事<br>(From Old to Latest Events) | 出来事や考え方が起こった順に、古いものから新しいものへと紹介します。 |
| 結論<br>(Conclusion) | 説明した出来事の重要なポイントを簡潔に要約します。 |

### 例

In the early 20th century, the world witnessed a series of significant technological advancements. One of the most notable breakthroughs was the invention of the automobile. In 1908, Henry Ford introduced the Model T, which revolutionized transportation. Shortly after, in 1914, the Panama Canal was completed, providing a vital shortcut for international trade. Finally, in 1917, the first transatlantic telephone call was made, connecting people across the ocean like never before. These events marked a remarkable era of progress and innovation.

下線部のようなシグナルワードで、時の流れ、事柄の起こった順序が年代順に示されています。このように、時系列順は出来事がどのように展開していったかを示すのに最適な方法です。

## 2　Cause and Effect ［原因・結果］

原因・結果の論理展開とは、特定の出来事や状況がどのような理由で発生したか（原因）と、その結果として何が起こったか（結果）を明確に示す方法です。このアプローチは、物事の因果関係を理解するために非常に有効です。原因・結果の論理展開は、複雑な問題を解き明かし、聴衆にその問題の背景と影響を理解させるのに役立ちます。

| 基本構造 | |
| --- | --- |
| 導入<br>(Introduction) | 因果関係を議論するトピックの紹介します。 |
| 原因<br>(Cause) | 出来事や状況が発生した理由や要因を説明します。 |
| 結果<br>(Effect) | その原因が引き起こした結果や影響を説明します。 |
| 結論<br>(Conclusion) | 議論した因果関係について簡潔にまとめます。 |

### 例

The Industrial Revolution brought about significant environmental consequences. The widespread use of coal and the establishment of factories led to increased air pollution. The release of harmful pollutants into the atmosphere resulted in the deterioration of air quality, contributing to respiratory problems and other health issues in nearby communities. Additionally, the discharge of industrial waste into water bodies led to water pollution, harming aquatic ecosystems and jeopardizing the availability of clean water for human consumption.

下線部のようなシグナルワードで因果関係を示しています。この例では、原因はthe industrial revolutionであり、その結果（影響）としてair and water pollution with associated health and ecological consequencesということが述べられています。

## 3 Problem-Solution ［問題解決］

問題解決型の論理展開とは、問題を特定し、その問題に対する解決策を提案する方法です。このアプローチは、問題の分析と解決策の提案を体系的に行うことで、聴衆に問題の理解とその解決方法を提供します。問題解決型の論理展開は、課題に直面したときに有効な戦略を示す際に特に役立ちます。

| 基本構造 | |
| --- | --- |
| 導入（Introduction） | 問題となるトピックを紹介します。 |
| 問題の特定<br>(Identifying the Problem) | 問題の概要とその重要性を説明します。 |
| 原因の分析<br>(Analyzing the Causes) | 問題の原因を掘り下げて分析します。 |
| 解決策の提案<br>(Proposing Solutions) | 問題を解決するための具体的な方法や戦略を提案します。 |
| 実行計画と効果の予測<br>(Implementation and Expected Outcomes) | 提案した解決策の実行方法と期待される効果を説明します。 |
| 結論（Conclusion） | 問題についての議論を簡潔にまとめます。 |

**例**

The issue of plastic pollution in our oceans has reached alarming levels. Plastic waste poses a significant threat to marine life, as animals often mistake it for food or become entangled in it. To address this problem, governments and communities can implement several solutions. Firstly, stricter regulations can be put in place to limit the use of single-use plastics and encourage the adoption of sustainable alternatives. Secondly, public awareness campaigns can educate individuals about the importance of responsible waste disposal and recycling. Lastly, supporting initiatives to develop innovative recycling technologies and infrastructure can help reduce the amount of plastic waste entering our oceans. By implementing these solutions, we can mitigate the problem of plastic pollution and protect our marine ecosystems.

このように、問題解決型の論理展開を使用することで、聴衆に対して問題の深刻さとその解決方法を明確に伝えることができます。

## 4 Compare and Contrast ［比較対照］

比較対照の論理展開とは、二つ以上の物事や概念を比較し、その類似点や相違点を明確に示す方法です。このアプローチは、特定のトピックについての理解を深め、異なる視点やアプローチを評価するのに役立ちます。比較対照の論理展開は、選択肢の分析や評価、異なる理論の比較などにおいて特に有効です。

| 基本構造 | |
|---|---|
| 導入<br>(Introduction) | 比較する対象とその重要性を紹介します。 |
| 類似点<br>(Similarities) | 比較する対象の共通点を説明します。 |
| 相違点<br>(Differences) | 比較する対象の違いを説明します。 |
| 結論<br>(Conclusion) | 主なポイントをまとめ、どちらがより優れているか、またはそれぞれの価値を強調します。 |

### 例

Comparing traditional education with online education reveals significant differences. Traditional education takes place in physical classrooms with face-to-face interaction between students and teachers, promoting immediate feedback and social interaction. On the other hand, online education offers flexibility in terms of time and location, allowing learners to access course materials and lectures at their convenience. In traditional education, students often follow a predetermined curriculum, whereas online education may offer more self-paced and customizable learning experiences. While traditional education provides a structured learning environment, online education encourages self-discipline and independence. Ultimately, the choice between the two depends on individual learning styles, preferences, and circumstances.

比較対照の構造を用いることで、異なる選択肢やコンセプトを効果的に分析し、それらの類似点や相違点を包括的に理解することができます。

## 5 Classification［分類］

分類の論理展開とは、特定のテーマやトピックを共通の特徴や基準に基づいてさまざまなグループやクラスに分ける方法です。このアプローチは、複雑な情報を整理し、体系的に提示する際に有効です。分類の論理展開は、聴衆が特定の分野における異なるカテゴリーを理解し、それぞれの特徴を明確にするのに役立ちます。

| 基本構造 | |
| --- | --- |
| 導入<br>(Introduction) | トピックの概要とその分類の重要性を紹介します。 |
| 分類基準<br>(Criteria for Classification) | 分類の基準を説明します。 |
| 各分類の説明<br>(Explanation of Each Category) | 各カテゴリーを詳細に説明し、その特徴を述べます。 |
| 結論<br>(Conclusion) | 各カテゴリーの要点をまとめ、分類の全体像を評価します。 |

### 例

Cuisine can be classified into different regional categories, each with its own distinct flavors and cooking techniques. Asian cuisine encompasses Chinese, Japanese, Thai, and Indian dishes, known for their use of spices, stir-frying, and unique flavor profiles. Mediterranean cuisine includes Greek, Italian, and Spanish dishes, featuring ingredients like olive oil, fresh vegetables, and herbs. Latin American cuisine incorporates Mexican, Brazilian, and Argentinian flavors, known for their bold spices, corn-based dishes, and grilled meats. Each regional classification showcases the culinary traditions and cultural heritage of a specific area.

分類の論理展開を使えば、複雑な情報を効果的に整理して提示することができ、さまざまなグループやその特徴を理解しやすくなります。

## 6 Definition ［定義］

定義の論理展開とは、用語、概念、アイディアの意味や意義を明確にし、具体的な説明や例を用いて理解を深める方法です。このアプローチは、特定のトピックについての基本的な定義や意味の理解を提供し、誤解を避けるために非常に重要です。定義の論理展開は、複雑な概念や専門用語を解説する際に特に有効です。

| 基本構造 | |
| --- | --- |
| 導入<br>(Introduction) | 定義する用語や概念を紹介し、その重要性を述べます。 |
| 基本的な定義<br>(Basic Definition) | 用語や概念の基本的な意味を説明します。 |
| 詳細な説明<br>(Detailed Explanation) | 定義の背景や関連する特徴、特性を詳しく説明します。 |
| 例<br>(Examples) | 実際の例を挙げて、定義がどのように適用されるかを示します。 |
| 結論<br>(Conclusion) | 主なポイントをまとめ、定義の重要性を強調します。 |

**例**

Friendship is a deep and meaningful connection between two individuals characterized by mutual affection, trust, and support. It is a voluntary relationship that goes beyond mere acquaintanceship, as friends share common interests, values, and experiences. Friends provide emotional support, companionship, and a sense of belonging. For example, they offer a safe space for sharing thoughts, feelings, and experiences without judgment. Genuine friendship is built on trust, honesty, and loyalty, and it plays a vital role in enhancing one's well-being and overall quality of life.

定義の論理展開を使って複雑な用語や概念を明確に説明することで、聴衆はその意味や意義を理解しやすくなります。

## 7　Descriptive ［説明］

説明の論理展開とは、人物、場所、物、出来事について生き生きとした言葉や感覚的な詳細を用いて描写する方法です。このアプローチは、聴衆に強い印象を与え、視覚、聴覚、嗅覚、触覚、味覚などの感覚を通じて鮮明なイメージを想起させることを目的としています。説明の論理展開は、感情や雰囲気を伝えるのに特に効果的です。

| 基本構造 | |
| --- | --- |
| 導入<br>(Introduction) | 説明する対象を紹介し、その説明の目的や重要性を述べます。 |
| 全体像の説明<br>(Overall Description) | 対象の全体的な特徴や印象を簡単に述べます。 |
| 詳細な描写<br>(Detailed Description) | 感覚的な詳細や具体的な特徴を順を追って説明します。 |
| 結論<br>(Conclusion) | 主なポイントをまとめ、説明の意義や印象を再確認します。 |

### 例

The old library was a haven of quiet and knowledge, its tall wooden shelves filled with dusty tomes that reached up to the high, ornate ceiling. Soft, golden light filtered through the stained glass windows, casting colorful patterns on the worn wooden floor. The scent of aged paper and leather bindings mingled with the faint aroma of polished wood, creating a comforting, nostalgic atmosphere. As I walked through the aisles, the gentle rustling of pages and the occasional creak of the floorboards were the only sounds, adding to the serene and contemplative atmosphere of this timeless place.

説明の論理展開を使えば、生き生きとした魅力的な描写ができ、聴衆が感覚を通して対象を体験できるため、より没入感のあるインパクトのあるプレゼンテーションになります。

## 8 Argumentative［議論］

議論の論理展開とは、明確なテーマや主張を提示し、それを証拠や論理的な推論でサポートすることで、特定の立場や視点に対する説得力のある意見を提示する方法です。このアプローチは、聴衆を説得し、自分の見解を支持させるために重要です。議論の論理展開では、論理的な推論、事実、統計、専門家の意見など、さまざまな証拠を用います。

| 基本構造 | |
|---|---|
| 導入<br>(Introduction) | 論点の概要と主張を明確に述べます。背景情報や問題の重要性を説明することも含まれます。 |
| 論点の提示<br>(Presentation of Arguments) | 主張をサポートするための主要な論点をいくつか挙げ、それぞれについて詳しく説明します。 |
| 反論の予測と反駁<br>(Counterarguments and Refutations) | 反対意見を予測し、それに対する反論を述べます。 |
| 証拠の提示<br>(Presentation of Evidence) | 各論点を支持するための証拠を具体的に示します。 |
| 結論<br>(Conclusion) | 主なポイントをまとめ、再度主張を強調し、聴衆に対する呼びかけや行動の提案を行います。 |

### 例

The use of cell phones in classrooms should be strictly prohibited. Cell phones are a major source of distraction, diverting students' attention from learning. Students often engage in texting, social media, or gaming during class, hindering their ability to focus. Additionally, incoming calls and notifications can disrupt the flow of lessons. While some argue that cell phones can serve as educational tools and provide emergency communication, these benefits are outweighed by the distractions they cause. Schools can offer alternative resources and communication methods, such as school-provided tablets and clear emergency protocols. By banning cell phones, schools can create a better learning environment, encouraging participation and minimizing distractions, ultimately enhancing academic performance.

議論の論理展開を用いれば、自分の見解に十分な裏付けがあり論理的な事例を提示することで、聴衆を効果的に説得することができます。

# 9 Process Analysis [手順分析]

手順分析の論理展開とは、複雑な手順をより小さなステップに分解し、各ステップを論理的な順序で説明し、聴衆が手順を理解し再現できるようにする方法です。このアプローチは、特定のタスクや作業の実行方法を明確にするのに役立ちます。手順分析は、料理レシピ、技術手順、学習方法の説明など、さまざまな分野で使用されます。

| 基本構造 | |
|---|---|
| 導入<br>(Introduction) | 分析する手順の背景を説明し、その重要性や目的を述べます。 |
| ステップの分解<br>(Breakdown of Steps) | 手順を細かいステップに分割し、それぞれのステップを論理的な順序で列挙します。 |
| 各ステップの説明<br>(Explanation of Each Step) | 各ステップを詳しく説明し、その目的や実行方法を示します。 |
| 結論<br>(Conclusion) | 手順の実行に必要なポイントをまとめ、聴衆に再現可能な手順を提供します。 |

**例**

To make a delicious homemade pizza, follow these simple steps. First, prepare the pizza dough by combining flour, yeast, salt, and water in a mixing bowl. Knead the dough until it becomes smooth and elastic. Then, let it rise in a warm place for about an hour until it doubles in size. Next, preheat the oven to the desired temperature and roll out the dough into a thin crust on a lightly floured surface. Place the rolled dough on a baking sheet or pizza stone. Now, it's time to add your favorite toppings, such as tomato sauce, cheese, and assorted vegetables or meats. Bake the pizza in the preheated oven for approximately 12-15 minutes or until the crust is golden and the cheese is melted and bubbly. Finally, remove the pizza from the oven, let it cool for a few minutes, and then slice and serve. Enjoy your homemade pizza!

手順の論理展開は、複雑な手順を細かいステップに分解し、それを論理的な順序で説明することで、聴衆が手順を理解しやすくなります。

## 10 Rhetorical Analysis [修辞学的分析]

修辞学的分析の論理展開とは、スピーチや文章を詳しく調べて、どのように説得力を持たせたり、メッセージを効果的に伝えたりしているかを分析する方法です。このアプローチは、書かれたものや話されたことを深く理解し、話し手や書き手がどのようにして聞き手や読み手を納得させようとしているかを知ることができます。修辞学的分析は、文学、歴史、政治、広告など、さまざまな分野で応用されます。

| 基本構造 | |
| --- | --- |
| 導入<br>(Introduction) | 分析するスピーチや文章などの背景や、話し手や書き手の意図を紹介し、分析の重要性を説明します。 |
| 修辞学的要素の分析<br>(Analysis of Rhetorical Elements) | スピーチや文章に使用されている説得力のあるテクニックや修辞法、言語的手法を検討します。 |
| 効果の評価<br>(Evaluation of Effects) | 使用された修辞学的要素がどのように聞き手や読み手に影響を与えるかを評価します。 |
| 結論<br>(Conclusion) | 修辞学的分析の結果をまとめ、その説得力や効果についての洞察を提供します。 |

### 例

In Martin Luther King Jr.'s famous speech, "I Have a Dream," he masterfully employs various rhetorical devices to convey his message of equality and justice. King's use of vivid imagery, such as the powerful metaphor of "sweltering summer of the Negro's legitimate discontent," creates a sensory experience that resonates with the audience and emphasizes the urgency of the civil rights movement. Additionally, his repetition of the phrase "I have a dream" throughout the speech serves as a powerful refrain, highlighting his vision of a future where racial discrimination is eradicated. Furthermore, King's skillful use of rhetorical questions engages the audience and prompts them to reflect on the moral implications of racial injustice. Through his effective utilization of these rhetorical devices, King captivates his listeners and inspires them to join the fight for equality.

修辞学的分析の論理展開を行うことで、聴衆は分析したスピーチや文章をより深く理解することができ、話し手や書き手の意図やメッセージをより正確に捉えることができます。

## 11 Inductive Reasoning ［帰納法］

帰納推論は、特定の事例や観察から一般的な原則や法則を導き出す推論の方法です。具体的な事例から一般的な結論を導く過程で、帰納的な論理展開が行われます。

| 基本構造 | |
|---|---|
| **観察や実験の事例の収集**<br>(Data Collection Based on Observation or Experiment) | 特定の事象や現象を観察し、それに関するデータや事例を集めます。 |
| **パターンや共通点の抽出**<br>(Extraction of Common Features of Patterns) | 収集した事例やデータから、共通するパターンや特徴を抽出します。 |
| **一般化の仮説の提案**<br>(Proposing Generalization Hypotheses) | 抽出したパターンや共通点をもとに、一般的な法則や原則を説明する仮説を立てます。 |
| **仮説の検証**<br>(Verification of Hypotheses) | 新しい事例やデータを使って仮説が正しいかどうかを確認します。もし仮説が正しければ、それを一般化して法則や原則として受け入れることができます。 |

### 例

Over the past five years, we have carefully monitored the migration patterns of birds in our region. In 2019, we noted that the majority of the songbirds arrived in early April, with warblers and thrushes being the first to appear. The following year, in 2020, the same pattern was observed: the songbirds, including warblers and thrushes, arrived in early April. In 2021 and 2022, despite slight variations in weather conditions, the arrival times remained consistent, with the songbirds making their appearance in early April. This year, in 2023, once again, the songbirds arrived in early April. Based on these consistent observations over five years, we can reasonably conclude that songbirds in our region typically migrate and arrive in early April each year.

このように帰納法推論では、特定の事例や観察から一般的な原則や法則を導き出します。

## 12　Deductive Reasoning ［演繹法］

演繹推論は、一般的な原則や法則から特定の事例や結論を導き出す推論の方法です。具体的な事実や前提から一般的な結論を導く過程で、演繹的な論理展開が行われます。

| | 基本構造 |
|---|---|
| 前提の設定<br>（Setting Assumptions） | 特定の前提や仮定を設定します。<br>例：「すべてのAはBである」 |
| 論理的な推論の適用<br>（Application of Logical Reasoning） | 前提に基づいて論理的な推論を行います。<br>例：「CはAである」という事実から「CはBである」と推論します。 |
| 結論の確認<br>（Confirmation of Conclusions） | 導き出した結論が前提と整合しているか確認します。<br>例：「すべてのAはBである」および「CはAである」から「CはBである」という結論を確認します。これにより、演繹推論が正当かどうかを評価します。 |

**例**

All mammals have a backbone. This characteristic is a defining feature of the mammalian class in the animal kingdom. Furthermore, all mammals are warm-blooded, meaning they maintain a constant body temperature regardless of the external environment. Dolphins, being mammals, must therefore have a backbone and be warm-blooded. Consequently, if we observe an animal with these traits—having a backbone and being warm-blooded—we can reasonably conclude that it is a mammal. Thus, the dolphin in the marine exhibit, which shows both of these characteristics, can be classified as a mammal.

このように、演繹推論は一般的な法則や原則から具体的な結論を導き出す方法として用いられます。

# 論理展開別有用表現 (Useful Expressions and Phrases)

## 1 Chronological (Time) Order [時系列順]

### Introducing the Topic

- [ ] Today, I will be discussing…
- [ ] The focus of my presentation is…
- [ ] I will present the information in chronological order…

### Beginning a Sequence

- [ ] Firstly, let's start with…
- [ ] To begin with…
- [ ] The initial stage/phase…

### Continuing a Sequence

- [ ] Moving on to…
- [ ] Next, we have…
- [ ] Following that…
- [ ] Subsequently…

### Signaling Progression

- [ ] As we move forward in time…
- [ ] With the passage of time…
- [ ] Over the course of…
- [ ] During this period…

### Highlighting a Transition or Shift

- [ ] At this point…
- [ ] Now, let's turn our attention to…
- [ ] A significant change occurred when…

## Describing Simultaneous Events

☐ Meanwhile…

☐ Concurrently…

☐ At the same time…

## Summarizing or Concluding a Period

☐ To summarize this stage…

☐ In conclusion for this phase…

☐ To wrap up this part…

## Indicating a Shift to the Next Stage

☐ Moving forward/onto the next phase…

☐ Transitioning to the following stage…

☐ Shifting our focus to…

## Presenting the Final Stage or Conclusion

☐ Finally, we come to…

☐ In the end…

☐ Lastly…

☐ To conclude…

## Conveying Time Frames

☐ In the beginning…

☐ During the early stages…

☐ Over the course of a few years…

☐ In the later part/phase…

☐ Towards the end…

## 2 Cause and Effect [原因・結果]

### Introducing the Topic

☐ Today, I will be discussing the cause and effect relationship between…

☐ The focus of my presentation is to explore the causes and effects of…

☐ I will present the information in terms of cause and effect…

### Introducing a Cause

☐ One of the primary causes of…

☐ A significant factor contributing to…

☐ One reason behind…

☐ An important catalyst for…

### Indicating Multiple Causes

☐ There are several factors that contribute to…

☐ A combination of factors leads to…

☐ Multiple elements play a role in…

### Describing the Effect

☐ As a result of…

☐ This leads to…

☐ Consequently…

☐ Therefore…

### Demonstrating a Direct Cause and Effect Relationship

☐ The cause-and-effect relationship is evident when…

☐ This directly impacts…

☐ The consequence of this is…

## Explaining a Chain of Causation

- [ ] This factor triggers…
- [ ] Which, in turn, leads to…
- [ ] This sets off a series of events that ultimately results in…

## Clarifying Causation and Correlation

- [ ] It's important to distinguish between causation and correlation…
- [ ] While there is a correlation between…, the causal link can be attributed to…
- [ ] The evidence suggests a causal relationship rather than a mere correlation.

## Presenting Supporting Evidence

- [ ] Studies have shown that…
- [ ] Statistical data indicates that…
- [ ] Examples from real-world scenarios demonstrate the cause and effect relationship…

## Summarizing Cause and Effect

- [ ] To summarize the causes…
- [ ] In conclusion, the primary effects…
- [ ] In summary, the evidence points to a strong cause and effect relationship…

## Discussing Long-term Effects and Implications

- [ ] The long-term consequences of…
- [ ] This has significant implications for…
- [ ] The effects of this can be seen in…

## 3 Problem-Solution [問題解決]

### Introducing the Problem

- [ ] Today, I will be addressing a significant problem that…
- [ ] The focus of my presentation is to propose solutions for…
- [ ] I will present a problem-solving approach to tackle…

### Describing the Problem

- [ ] The main issue at hand is…
- [ ] We are faced with a complex problem of…
- [ ] The problem arises from…

### Identifying the Underlying Causes

- [ ] One of the root causes behind this problem is…
- [ ] Several factors contribute to the emergence of this issue, such as…
- [ ] The problem can be attributed to…

### Presenting Evidence and Data

- [ ] Studies have shown that…
- [ ] Statistical data supports the existence of this problem…
- [ ] Examples from real-world scenarios illustrate the extent of the problem…

### Proposing a Solution

- [ ] One potential way to address this problem is…
- [ ] A promising approach to tackle this issue involves…
- [ ] I would like to suggest…

## Outlining the Steps of the Solution

☐ The first step in the proposed solution is…

☐ Next, we need to…

☐ Following that, we can…

## Providing a Rationale

☐ This solution is effective because…

☐ By implementing this approach, we can…

☐ The chosen method takes into account…

## Discussing Potential Challenges

☐ However, we should be aware of potential challenges, such as…

☐ One obstacle we may face in implementing this solution is…

☐ It's important to address the potential drawbacks, including…

## Offering Alternatives or Variations

☐ Another possible solution to consider is…

☐ In addition to the proposed solution, an alternative approach could be…

☐ We could also explore variations of this method, such as…

## Concluding and Summarizing

☐ To summarize the proposed solution…

☐ In conclusion, the suggested approach…

☐ Ultimately, by implementing these solutions, we can work toward resolving the problem…

## 4 Compare and Contrast [比較対照]

### Introducing the Topic

- ☐ Today, I will be comparing and contrasting…
- ☐ The focus of my presentation is to examine the similarities and differences of…
- ☐ I will present a comparative analysis of…

### Stating the Similarities

- ☐ Both [A] and [B] share similarities in terms of…
- ☐ There are several commonalities between [A] and [B], such as…
- ☐ Both [A] and [B] exhibit…

### Highlighting Differences

- ☐ On the other hand, [A] and [B] differ in terms of…
- ☐ A notable contrast between [A] and [B] is…
- ☐ Unlike [A], [B] displays…

### Pointing Out Specific Aspects for Comparison

- ☐ When comparing [X] of [A] and [B]…
- ☐ In terms of [Y], there are notable differences between [A] and [B]…
- ☐ An interesting point of comparison is…

### Drawing Parallels

- ☐ It is interesting to note the similarities between [A] and [B] in regard to…
- ☐ A parallel can be drawn between [A] and [B] when it comes to…
- ☐ Both [A] and [B] demonstrate a commonality in…

## Contrasting Viewpoints or Perspectives

- [ ] While [A] takes a more [X], [B] adopts a different approach, namely [Y]…
- [ ] In terms of [Z], [A] and [B] hold contrasting opinions…
- [ ] The differing perspectives of [A] and [B] become evident when considering…

## Presenting Supporting Evidence

- [ ] Research studies provide evidence for the similarities between [A] and [B] by showing…
- [ ] Statistical data highlights the differences in terms of…
- [ ] Examples from real-world scenarios illustrate the comparative aspects…

## Analyzing the Implications

- [ ] These similarities suggest that…
- [ ] The differences between [A] and [B] have important implications, such as…
- [ ] By comparing and contrasting [A] and [B], we gain insights into…

## Discussing Significance and Relevance

- [ ] Understanding the similarities and differences between [A] and [B] is crucial for…
- [ ] This comparative analysis is relevant because it sheds light on…
- [ ] By examining the comparisons and contrasts, we can better grasp…

## Concluding and Summarizing

- [ ] To summarize the comparison…
- [ ] In conclusion, the similarities and differences between [A] and [B] highlight…
- [ ] Ultimately, this comparative analysis provides a comprehensive understanding of…

## 5 Classification [分類]

### Introducing the Topic

- ☐ Today, I will be discussing the classification of…
- ☐ The focus of my presentation is to explore the different categories of…
- ☐ I will present a classification framework for…

### Stating the Overarching Categories

- ☐ The primary classification consists of…
- ☐ There are several main categories within…
- ☐ The classification can be broadly divided into…

### Describing the Criteria for Classification

- ☐ The classification is based on specific criteria, such as…
- ☐ We categorize [A] and [B] according to…
- ☐ The classification takes into account factors such as…

### Presenting Subcategories

- ☐ Within the broader category of [X], we can identify subcategories including…
- ☐ The classification further branches out into subgroups, namely…
- ☐ When examining [Y], we can observe subcategories such as…

### Explaining the Characteristics of Each Category

- ☐ [A] is characterized by…
- ☐ The distinguishing features of [B] include…
- ☐ Each category within the classification exhibits unique traits, such as…

## Providing Examples

☐ To illustrate the classification, let's consider the following examples…

☐ For instance, within the category of [A], we can find examples such as…

☐ Examples from real-world scenarios exemplify the different categories, such as…

## Discussing Similarities within Categories

☐ One commonality among the categories is…

☐ All the categories share the characteristic of…

☐ There are notable similarities within the classification, particularly in terms of…

## Addressing Overlaps or Borderline Cases

☐ Some instances may blur the boundaries between categories, as they possess characteristics of both…

☐ In certain cases, the classification may encounter overlaps, particularly when considering…

☐ There can be borderline cases that exhibit traits from multiple categories, such as…

## Analyzing the Significance of the Classification

☐ This classification framework provides a comprehensive understanding of…

☐ By categorizing [A] and [B], we gain insights into…

☐ The classification is valuable for its ability to…

## Concluding and Summarizing

☐ To summarize the classification…

☐ In conclusion, the classification framework offers a systematic approach to…

☐ Ultimately, this classification allows us to organize and comprehend…

## 6　Definition ［定義］

### Introducing the Topic

- ☐ Today, I will be discussing the definition of…
- ☐ The focus of my presentation is to provide a clear definition for…
- ☐ I will present a comprehensive definition of…

### Presenting a Formal Definition

- ☐ According to [source/expert], [term] is defined as…
- ☐ A widely accepted definition of [term] is…
- ☐ In academic literature, [term] is commonly defined as…

### Providing a Concise Explanation

- ☐ In simple terms, [term] can be defined as…
- ☐ Essentially, [term] refers to…
- ☐ At its core, [term] means…

### Clarifying Key Components or Attributes

- ☐ The definition of [term] includes the following key components:…
- ☐ When we talk about [term], we are referring to…
- ☐ A fundamental aspect of [term] is…

### Describing the Scope or Boundaries

- ☐ The definition of [term] encompasses…
- ☐ The concept of [term] applies to…
- ☐ It is important to note the boundaries of [term], which include…

## Addressing Variations or Alternative Definitions

☐ While there are variations in the way [term] is defined, a common understanding is…

☐ Different perspectives on [term] may offer alternative definitions, such as…

☐ It's worth considering alternative definitions of [term], which include…

## Exploring Historical or Contextual Definitions

☐ Throughout history, the definition of [term] has evolved, initially referring to…

☐ The meaning of [term] has shifted over time, from its earlier definition of…

☐ The definition of [term] can be understood in the context of…

## Highlighting the Significance of the Definition

☐ A clear definition of [term] is crucial for…

☐ By providing a precise definition, we can better understand…

☐ The definition of [term] is important because it helps to…

## Relating the Definition to Broader Concepts

☐ The definition of [term] is closely related to the concept of…

☐ Understanding [term] is essential for grasping the broader concept of…

☐ By defining [term], we gain insights into the broader framework of…

## Concluding and Summarizing

☐ To summarize the definition of [term]…

☐ In conclusion, the definition of [term] encompasses…

☐ Ultimately, a clear and comprehensive definition of [term] allows us to…

## 7 Descriptive [Descriptive]

### Introducing the Topic

- ☐ Today, I will be providing a detailed description of…
- ☐ The focus of my presentation is to describe…
- ☐ I will present a comprehensive overview of…

### Setting the Context

- ☐ In order to understand [subject], it is important to have a clear description of…
- ☐ Before delving into the specifics, let me provide you with a brief description of…
- ☐ To begin, let's establish a general description of…

### Providing a General Overview

- ☐ At its core, [subject] can be described as…
- ☐ In broad terms, [subject] refers to…
- ☐ In simple words, [subject] can be defined as…

### Utilizing Sensory Details

- ☐ When we think of [subject], we imagine…
- ☐ The sight of [subject] is characterized by…
- ☐ One can easily recognize [subject] through its distinct smell/sound/taste…

### Breaking Down the Components

- ☐ In terms of its structure, [subject] is composed of…
- ☐ The main elements that constitute [subject] are…
- ☐ We can identify several key components of [subject], including…

## Describing Characteristics and Features

☐ One notable characteristic of [subject] is…

☐ The distinguishing features of [subject] include…

☐ Among its notable features, [subject] displays…

## Exploring Variations and Types

☐ There are several variations/types of [subject], such as…

☐ Within the broader category of [subject], we can find different types including…

☐ When it comes to [subject], there are several distinct variations, namely…

## Discussing Historical or Cultural Significance

☐ Throughout history, [subject] has played a significant role in…

☐ In various cultures, [subject] holds a special significance, symbolizing…

☐ The historical context of [subject] sheds light on its cultural importance…

## Providing Examples

☐ To illustrate the description of [subject], consider the following examples…

☐ For instance, when we encounter [subject], we can observe examples such as…

☐ Examples from real-world scenarios exemplify the characteristics of [subject], such as…

## Concluding and Summarizing

☐ To summarize the description of [subject]…

☐ In conclusion, the comprehensive description of [subject] reveals…

☐ Ultimately, through this detailed description, we gain a thorough understanding of…

## 8 Argumentative [議論]

### Introducing the Topic

- ☐ Today, I will be presenting a compelling argument regarding…
- ☐ The focus of my presentation is to argue for/against…
- ☐ I will present a strong case in support of/opposition to…

### Stating Your Thesis or Main Argument

- ☐ My thesis is that…
- ☐ I firmly believe that…
- ☐ The main argument I will be making is…

### Presenting Supporting Evidence

- ☐ Research studies have consistently shown that…
- ☐ Statistical data supports the claim that…
- ☐ Examples from real-world scenarios illustrate the validity of…

### Citing Authoritative Sources

- ☐ According to [expert/source],…
- ☐ Renowned scholars in the field argue that…
- ☐ In a study conducted by [researcher], it was found that…

### Providing Logical Reasoning

- ☐ The logical reasoning behind this argument includes…
- ☐ The evidence leads to the conclusion that…
- ☐ By applying deductive reasoning, we can conclude that…

## Addressing Counterarguments

☐ Some may argue that [counterargument], but…

☐ It is important to consider the counterargument that…

☐ While there may be objections to this argument, the evidence suggests that…

## Refuting Counterarguments

☐ However, this counterargument fails to consider…

☐ The evidence contradicts the notion that…

☐ A closer examination reveals the flaws in the counterargument that…

## Offering Alternative Perspectives

☐ Another perspective to consider is…

☐ An alternative viewpoint suggests that…

☐ There are those who argue for a different approach, namely…

## Anticipating and Addressing Potential Objections

☐ One potential objection to this argument is…

☐ It is important to address the potential criticism that…

☐ To preempt potential objections, it should be noted that…

## Concluding and Summarizing

☐ In conclusion, the evidence and logical reasoning support the argument that…

☐ To summarize the argument…

☐ Ultimately, this argument presents a compelling case for…

## 9 Process Analysis [手順分析]

### Introducing the Topic

- [ ] Today, I will be providing a detailed analysis of the process of…
- [ ] The focus of my presentation is to examine the steps involved in…
- [ ] I will present a comprehensive overview of the process of…

### Describing the Purpose of the Process

- [ ] The process of [process name] serves the purpose of…
- [ ] The primary goal of this process is to…
- [ ] This process is essential for achieving…

### Outlining the Steps of the Process

- [ ] The process can be broken down into the following steps:…
- [ ] There are several sequential stages involved in this process, including…
- [ ] To understand the process, let's examine the step-by-step procedure of...

### Using Transitional Phrases to Indicate Sequence

- [ ] Firstly, let's start with...
- [ ] Next, we move on to...
- [ ] Once [step A] is completed, we proceed to...

### Providing Detailed Explanations for Each Step

- [ ] During [step A], the purpose is to...
- [ ] At [step B], it is crucial to...
- [ ] One important aspect of [step C] is...

## Describing the Tools or Resources Required

☐ To carry out this process, certain tools are necessary, such as...

☐ In order to successfully complete [step A], specific resources are needed, including...

☐ The process relies on the use of equipment such as...

## Explaining Potential Challenges or Considerations

☐ Throughout the process, it is important to be aware of potential challenges, such as...

☐ Certain factors need to be taken into consideration at different stages, including...

☐ One challenge that may arise during this process is...

## Addressing Variations or Alternative Approaches

☐ While the presented process is widely used, alternative approaches include...

☐ In certain contexts, variations of this process may involve...

☐ It's worth noting that there can be different methods for carrying out this process, such as...

## Highlighting the Significance or Benefits of the Process

☐ This process is significant because it allows for...

☐ By following this process, one can benefit from...

☐ The advantages of using this process include...

## Concluding and Summarizing

☐ To summarize the process analysis...

☐ In conclusion, the detailed analysis of this process reveals...

☐ Ultimately, understanding the step-by-step procedure of this process enables us to...

## 10  Rhetorical Analysis [修辞学的分析]

## Introducing the Topic

☐ Today, I will be conducting a rhetorical analysis of...

☐ The focus of my presentation is to examine the rhetorical strategies employed in...

☐ I will present a comprehensive analysis of the persuasive techniques used in...

## Identifying the Rhetorical Context

☐ To understand the rhetorical strategies, it is important to consider the context in which...

☐ Before delving into the analysis, let's establish the rhetorical context of...

☐ The rhetorical analysis of [text/speech] takes into account the audience, purpose, and context.

## Analyzing the Speaker's/Writer's Credibility

☐ The speaker/writer establishes credibility by...

☐ The use of expert opinions and credentials enhances the speaker's/writer's credibility.

☐ The speaker's/writer's ethos is reinforced through...

## Examining Persuasive Appeals (Ethos, Pathos, Logos)

**Ethos:**

☐ The speaker/writer appeals to the audience's trust by...

☐ The use of personal anecdotes and experiences enhances the speaker's ethos.

**Pathos:**

☐ The speaker/writer evokes emotions of…

☐ Through vivid imagery and powerful language, the audience is emotionally engaged.

**Logos:**

☐ The speaker/writer presents logical arguments by…

☐ The use of statistics and facts strengthens the logical appeal.

## Analyzing Rhetorical Devices

- [ ] The speaker/writer employs rhetorical devices such as…
- [ ] The use of metaphors, similes, and analogies enhances the persuasive impact.
- [ ] Repetition and parallelism are used to create a memorable and persuasive effect.

## Examining the Structure and Organization

- [ ] The speaker/writer follows a clear and strategic structure, starting with…
- [ ] Transitional phrases and cohesive elements guide the audience through the argument.
- [ ] The arrangement of ideas builds up to a compelling climax/conclusion.

## Identifying Tone and Style

- [ ] The speaker/writer adopts a persuasive tone of…
- [ ] The use of figurative language and rhetorical questions adds to the persuasive style.
- [ ] The tone transitions from… to… to evoke different responses from the audience.

## Analyzing the Intended Audience

- [ ] The speaker/writer tailors the rhetoric to appeal to the target audience of…
- [ ] The use of language and references aligns with the audience's values and beliefs.
- [ ] The rhetoric employs specific cultural references and shared experiences.

## Evaluating the Overall Effectiveness

- [ ] The rhetorical strategies employed effectively achieve the speaker's/writer's purpose of…
- [ ] The use of rhetorical devices and persuasive appeals contributes to the overall impact.
- [ ] The rhetoric successfully convinces the audience to…

## Concluding and Summarizing

- ☐ To summarize the rhetorical analysis…
- ☐ In conclusion, the analysis of [text/speech] reveals the strategic use of rhetorical devices, persuasive appeals, and stylistic elements to…
- ☐ Ultimately, the rhetorical analysis provides insights into the persuasive techniques employed to…

## 11 Inductive Reasoning [帰納法]

## Introducing the Topic

- ☐ Today, I will be presenting an inductive reasoning analysis regarding…
- ☐ The focus of my presentation is to draw conclusions based on specific observations in…
- ☐ I will present a comprehensive examination of the evidence to support an inductive argument for…

## Explaining the Concept of Inductive Reasoning

- ☐ Inductive reasoning involves drawing general conclusions based on specific observations.
- ☐ Inductive reasoning is a process of reasoning that moves from specific instances to general patterns or principles.
- ☐ By examining specific examples or evidence, we can derive broader conclusions through inductive reasoning.

## Presenting Specific Observations or Evidence

- ☐ The evidence suggests that…
- ☐ Several instances indicate that…
- ☐ Examples in the field of [topic] demonstrate that…

## Identifying Patterns or Trends

☐ Upon analyzing the data, a clear pattern emerges.

☐ Multiple instances show a consistent trend.

☐ The observations reveal a recurring pattern.

## Presenting a Hypothesis or Generalization

☐ Based on the evidence, we can hypothesize that…

☐ A generalization that can be drawn from the observations is…

☐ The pattern observed suggests a broader principle, which is…

## Highlighting the Strength of the Evidence

☐ The evidence is robust and consistent.

☐ Multiple sources and studies support the observed pattern.

☐ The observations are based on a large and diverse sample.

## Addressing Potential Limitations or Counterexamples

☐ While the observations support the generalization, it is important to consider potential exceptions.

☐ It should be noted that there may be counterexamples that challenge the general pattern.

☐ Further research is needed to examine if the observed pattern holds true in all cases.

## Discussing the Significance or Implications of the Inductive Reasoning

☐ The inductive reasoning analysis sheds light on…

☐ Understanding the broader implications of the observed pattern can contribute to…

☐ The findings have practical implications in the field of…

### Evaluating the Strength of the Inductive Argument

- [ ] The inductive argument is strong due to the consistency and coherence of the evidence.
- [ ] The observations provide persuasive support for the generalization.
- [ ] While the inductive reasoning is not absolute, it provides a strong basis for the conclusion.

### Concluding and Summarizing

- [ ] To summarize the inductive reasoning analysis…
- [ ] In conclusion, the examination of specific observations allows us to draw general conclusions regarding…
- [ ] Ultimately, the inductive reasoning analysis provides insights into the patterns and principles that can be derived from…

## 12 Deductive Reasoning [演繹法]

### Introducing the Topic

- [ ] Today, I will be presenting a deductive reasoning analysis regarding…
- [ ] The focus of my presentation is to draw logical conclusions based on premises in…
- [ ] I will present a comprehensive examination of the evidence to support a deductive argument for…

### Explaining the Concept of Deductive Reasoning

- [ ] Deductive reasoning involves drawing specific conclusions based on general principles or premises.
- [ ] In deductive reasoning, we move from general statements to specific instances or predictions.
- [ ] By applying deductive logic, we can derive specific implications or conclusions from broader principles.

## Stating the Premises or General Principles

☐ The premises upon which the deductive argument is based are...

☐ Given the general principles of [topic], we can deduce that...

☐ The starting point of the deductive reasoning is the premise that...

## Presenting Logical Connections

☐ The logical connection between the premises and the conclusion is...

☐ By following the deductive logic, we arrive at the conclusion that...

☐ The premises necessarily lead to the logical consequence that...

## Applying Syllogistic Reasoning

☐ The deductive argument follows a syllogistic structure, with the major premise that...

☐ The syllogism involves the minor premise that...

☐ By applying the rules of syllogistic reasoning, we can deduce that...

## Highlighting the Validity of the Argument

☐ The deductive argument is valid due to the logical structure and coherence of the premises.

☐ The conclusion necessarily follows from the given premises.

☐ The argument adheres to the principles of deductive reasoning, ensuring the validity of the conclusion.

## Addressing Potential Objections or Counterarguments

☐ While the deductive argument is valid, objections may arise regarding...

☐ It is important to consider potential counterexamples or exceptions to the general principles.

☐ Further examination is required to address potential weaknesses or limitations of the deductive reasoning.

### Discussing the Significance or Implications of the Deductive Reasoning

- [ ] The deductive reasoning analysis provides insights into…
- [ ] Understanding the logical implications of the argument can contribute to…
- [ ] The findings have theoretical or practical implications in the field of…

### Evaluating the Strength of the Deductive Argument

- [ ] The deductive argument is strong due to the logical structure and validity of the reasoning.
- [ ] The premises provide strong support for the conclusion, ensuring the soundness of the argument.
- [ ] While the deductive reasoning is not absolute, it provides a strong basis for the conclusion.

### Concluding and Summarizing

- [ ] To summarize the deductive reasoning analysis…
- [ ] In conclusion, the examination of the premises and logical connections allows us to draw specific conclusions regarding…
- [ ] Ultimately, the deductive reasoning analysis provides insights into the logical implications and consequences that can be derived from…

# Web動画のご案内 ***StreamLine***

本テキストの映像は、オンラインでのストリーミング再生になります。下記URLよりご利用ください。なお**有効期限は、はじめてログインした時点から1年半**です。

**http://st.seibido.co.jp**

**1 ログイン画面**

🔒 **LOGIN**

テキストに添付されているシールをはがして、
12桁のアクセスコードをご入力ください。

[ ] - [ ] - [ ]

同意してログイン

以下の「利用規約」をご確認頂き、同意する場合は
上記ボタン【同意してログイン】を押してください。

利用規約

1. このウェブサイト（以下「本サイト」といいます）は、
株式会社成美堂（以下「弊社」といいます）が運営しています。
弊社の商品・サービス（以下「本サービス」といいます）利用時の
会員登録の有無を問わず、本サイトの利用にあたっては、
以下のご利用条件をお読み頂き、これらの条件にご同意の上ご利用ください。

2. 本サービスに関して個別に利用規約がある場合、
本規約に加えそれらも適用されます。

3. 本サイトを通じて、弊社の商品を販売する第三者のウェブサイトに
ご案内ないしリンクされることがあります。
リンク先ウェブサイトにおいて提供された個人情報は

> 巻末に添付されている
> シールをはがして、ア
> クセスコードをご入
> 力ください。

**2 メニュー画面**

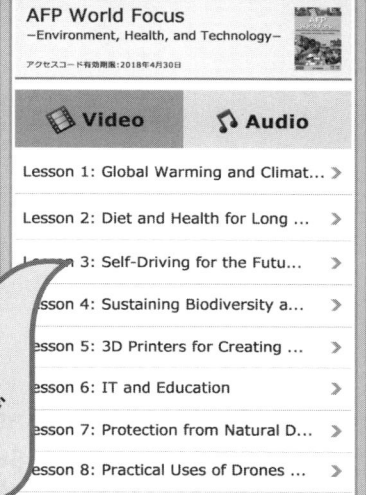

**AFP World Focus**
–Environment, Health, and Technology–

アクセスコード有効期限：2018年4月30日

🎬 **Video**     🎵 **Audio**

Lesson 1: Global Warming and Climat... ＞
Lesson 2: Diet and Health for Long ... ＞
Lesson 3: Self-Driving for the Futu... ＞
Lesson 4: Sustaining Biodiversity a... ＞
Lesson 5: 3D Printers for Creating ... ＞
Lesson 6: IT and Education ＞
Lesson 7: Protection from Natural D... ＞
Lesson 8: Practical Uses of Drones ... ＞

> 「**Video**」または
> 「**Audio**」を選択すると、
> それぞれストリーミング
> 再生ができます。

**3 再生画面**

**AFP World Focus**
–Environment, Health, and Technology–

アクセスコード有効期限：2018年4月30日

Lesson 2:
Diet and Health for Long Lives
食習慣：長生きのためのスーパーフードを探す

**推奨動作環境**

**【PC OS】**
Windows 7~  /  Mac 10.8~

**【Mobile OS】**
iOS / Android ※Android の場合は4.x~が推奨

**【Desktop ブラウザ】**
Internet Explorer 9~ / Firefox / Chrome / Safari

## TEXT PRODUCTION STAFF

edited by 編集
Takashi Kudo 工藤 隆志

book design by 装丁
Tomoyuki Adachi (parastyle inc.) 足立 友幸（有限会社パラスタイル）

typesetting by 組版
Midoriko Iio (parastyle inc.) 飯尾 緑子（有限会社パラスタイル）


## CD PRODUCTION STAFF

recorded by 吹き込み者
Rachel Walzer (AmE) レイチェル・ワルザー（アメリカ英語）
Howard Colefield (AmE) ハワード・コルフィールド（アメリカ英語）

## Deliver Your Message:
## Enhancing Presentation Skills with Videographics
## ビデオグラフィックスを活用した英語プレゼンテーション演習

2025年1月20日　初版発行
2025年2月15日　第2刷発行

編著者　　宍戸 真
　　　　　高橋 真理子
　　　　　Kevin Murphy

発行者　　佐野 英一郎

発行所　　株式会社 成 美 堂
　　　　　〒101-0052東京都千代田区神田小川町3-22
　　　　　TEL 03-3291-2261　　FAX 03-3293-5490
　　　　　https://www.seibido.co.jp

印刷・製本　三美印刷株式会社

ISBN 978-4-7919-7310-1　　　　　　　　　　　　Printed in Japan